NEW ZEALAND
GEOGRAPHIC

preceding pages:

ARNO GASTEIGER

Each summer, 1000 mad-keen anglers fling themselves into the surf of New Zealand's longest beach in the hope of landing "the big one" that will win them $50,000 in the Ninety Mile Beach Snapper Classic. Outdoor pursuits, whether on land or sea, are part of the New Zealand way of life.

GLENN JOWITT

Her smile as delicate as the flower ei she wears in her hair, a Cook Islands dancer prepares for a performance at the Gluepot Hotel in Auckland. Some 23,000 Cook Islanders have emigrated to New Zealand; 17,000 remain on their native islands.

KIM WESTERSKOV

Lithe and muscular, a pod of common dolphins easily keeps pace with the photographer's boat. This species of dolphin, one of several encountered around the coasts of New Zealand, is distinguishable by yellow markings on the flanks. One of the dolphins is releasing a stream of air bubbles as it "whistles."

ARNO GASTEIGER

The village pub is a focal point in small communities such as Puhoi, north of Auckland, where descendants of the area's Bohemian settlers keep alive the music of their forbears. Photographs and memorabilia remind patrons of Puhoi's history as a logging town.

following pages:

ARNO GASTEIGER

The term "adventure tourism" may be of recent origin, but the New Zealand wilderness has been attracting adventurers for generations. A group of rafters prepares to take a set of rapids in the Karamea River, in North-West Nelson.

DEREK GRZELEWSKI

Thrusting skyward from the mountainous spine of the South Island, New Zealand's tallest peak, Aoraki or Mt Cook, stands 3753 metres high, and was first climbed on Christmas Day 1894. Within the boundaries of Mt Cook National Park are 18 more peaks over 3000 metres in height, as well as several major glaciers.

GEOFF MASON

Kinship with the land and a desire to harvest its bounty are feelings deeply ingrained in many New Zealanders. Deer and pig hunting, duck shooting, fresh and salt water fishing—these are all strong New Zealand traditions.

following pages:

DARRYL TORCKLER

High tide brings a fresh input of plankton and nutrients—and a school of yellow-eyed mullet—to a mangrove-lined wetland in Northland. Mangroves are the amphibians of the plant world, content to be covered twice daily by the tide, and able to flourish where no other flowering trees can survive.

preceding pages:

MICHAEL SCHNEIDER

Determination and a gritty desire to beat the odds are a national characteristic. More gutsy than most, West Coast amputee Steve Maitland has competed three times in the country's legendary triathlon, the Coast to Coast—a 239-km cycle, kayak and run across the South Island.

ARNO GASTEIGER

"Do not hesitate, donate! For he who parts with a dollar or two parts also with sadness." Philosophy and the chalk-drawn face of one of the country's best-known bards help draw in some dollars for a Queen Street artist.

FRANCOIS MARITZ

Messing about in boats is a way of life in many parts of the country—particularly in the harbours of the North. Here Mrs Pepe Tito and friends of Tapora, on the Kaipara Harbour, head out for a spot of fishing.

ARNO GASTEIGER

The twisting harbour of Port Hardy, d'Urville Island, was the first taste of New Zealand for many 19th century immigrants. For them, the sight of the raw, elemental landscape must have tinged their hopes with trepidation; for many in this generation, such wild places serve as a haven from frantic urban life.

MICHAEL SCHNEIDER

With the eyes of a million yesterdays, New Zealand's great survivor (and New Zealand Geographic's *mascot) the tuatara has a lineage that extends back 200 million years to the age of dinosaurs. The reptile is literally in a class of its own; it exists nowhere else in the world.*

The journal of New Zealand

NEW ZEALAND GEOGRAPHIC

KENNEDY WARNE

David Bateman

NEW ZEALAND GEOGRAPHIC

BY   Kennedy Warne

PHOTOGRAPHIC AND
DESIGN ASSISTANT   Arno Gasteiger
EDITORIAL ASSISTANT   Warren Judd
PRODUCTION ASSISTANT   Glenn Conroy

CONTRIBUTORS

WRITERS   Nigel Cox
Alison Cree
Charles Daugherty
Gerard Hindmarsh
Raewyn Mackenzie
Buddy Mikaere
Mark Scott
Stefan Seitzer
Philip Temple
Vaughan Yarwood

PHOTOGRAPHERS   Andris Apse
Nathan Bilow
Will Cooper
Phil Crawford
Clare Cunningham
Andrew Dixon
Alan Dove
Gareth Eyres
Paul Fisher
Scott Freeman
Arno Gasteiger
Roger Grace
Derek Grzelewski
Alastair Jamieson
Leonie Johnsen
Glenn Jowitt
Ian MacDonald
Francois Maritz
Geoff Mason
David Mathieson
Roger Moffat
Peter Moore
Rod Morris
Dean Nixon
Geoff Osborne
Ruth Prendergast
Peter Quinn
Gordon Roberts
Stephen Roke
Mark Scott
Ralph Talmont
Darryl Torckler
Marcel Tromp
Kennedy Warne
Kim Westerskov
Miles Wislang

Published in 1995 by David Bateman Ltd, Tarndale Grove, Albany Business Park, Auckland, New Zealand, in association with N. Z. Geographic Publications Ltd, 110 Mt Eden Rd, Auckland, New Zealand.

Copyright © N. Z. Geographic Publications Ltd, 1995
Copyright © David Bateman Ltd, 1995

ISBN 1 86953 219 8

Printed in Hong Kong by Everbest Printing Co.

NEW ZEALAND GEOGRAPHIC

A journey to the centre of New Zealand

There were five of us watching for taiko that moonless October night. We were lying on potato sacks in the bracken, staring up at a sky scrubbed clean by a freezing southerly and alive with stars.

A halogen searchlight powered by generator thrust a pale yellow cone of light into the darkness, and gave some form to the Chatham Island valley where we were camped. There were two hours to midnight, and taiko—the magenta petrel, one of the rarest birds in the world—could arrive at any time.

Taiko come to this remote valley to breed, and each year a group of conservation scientists and volunteers stake out the area in an attempt to catch and band a few individuals.

Five pairs of eyes scanned the heavens, watching for movement. From time to time a shape would flutter through the halogen beam, causing a flurry of excitement—moths, other species of seabird, never a taiko.

Then, a few minutes after midnight, the longed-for bird suddenly materialised. The leader of the spotting team leaped to his feet and flicked on a hand-held spotlight. If he could hold the swooping, gliding form in its beam for long enough, the bird would become disoriented, tire and fall to the ground.

He played it masterfully, like a fisherman a marlin. At one point the taiko passed bare metres above our heads, its slender wings stretched wide, then dipped down behind a tree. Freed from the light for a second, it was able to reorient itself, and disappeared up the valley. The fish had thrown the hook.

We returned to our vigil, but no more taiko came that night. Nor on many other nights. During several weeks of all-night watches, only 12 were caught.

I marvelled at my luck. By torchlight on a starry night I had almost touched a ghostly bird which just 20 years ago was thought extinct. The experience was all that I had hoped for, but more than I deserved.

I feel the same way about six years of editing *New Zealand Geographic.*

When, in the winter of 1988, a friend suggested we publish a magazine which would do for New Zealand what *National Geographic* has done for the world, I had little concept of the journey on which I was embarking. But I was more than happy—literally and figuratively—to hang up my business suit and put on my walking shoes. To launch this kite called *New Zealand Geographic*, wind the string around my hand and hold on.

It's been quite an adventure.

Research for the over 120 subjects we have featured in the magazine has taken me underground to examine moa skeletons in Golden Bay and aloft by Navy helicopter to photograph the atolls of Tokelau. I have stalked tahr through snow and spike-leafed scrub and pukeko knee-deep through black swamp sediment. I have sorted shellfish on the pitching deck of an oyster boat in Foveaux Strait and studied lighthouse lenses in sweltering heat at Cape Reinga.

I consider the last six years to have been a trek towards the heart of New Zealand, one that has embraced geography, history, industry, popular culture, biology (my own special interest) and the lives of an extraordinary array of New Zealanders.

Along the way, I have realised the importance of making the most of each encounter with the natural world. Learning to observe, and to respond, and not just to pass by.

Thomas Carlyle said: "The man who cannot wonder is like a pair of spectacles behind which there are no eyes." That sense of wonder, so vivid in childhood, is all too easily eroded. The remedy is as simple as stepping outside and renewing a personal contract with nature. Study the clouds, smell the clematis, follow an ant trail, hear a weta rasping out its song. These are the doorways to wonder.

Happily, they are not beyond the reach of even the least adventurous New Zealander. A love of the forests, the mountains, the sea lies close to the surface of our collective identity. And just as well: to lose our connection with the land that supports us and with the creatures that draw breath alongside us is to be less than fully alive.

The author about to explore Mayor Island with a Ministry of Transport lighthouse maintenance crew.

New Zealand Geographic is about making that connection and about being surprised and enchanted by the marvel of what we discover.

"We are all travellers in the wilderness of this world, and the best that we find in our travels is an honest friend," wrote Robert Louis Stevenson.

My hope is that the reader will find in this volume, and in the magazine which gave it birth, such a friend.

The making of the magazine

KIM WESTERSKOV

Diver faces a five-metre-long humpback whale in clear tropical waters near Tonga. Such encounters are rare: frequent contributor Westerskov spent a month in the area, and this was the only close contact he experienced.

I t was one of those once-in-a-lifetime encounters which make all the planning and hard work worth while.

Tonga, September 1994. Underwater photographer Kim Westerskov had already spent one winter trying to photograph humpback whales. Now he was back for a second season: a month of criss-crossing the ocean following the whales, which congregate here to breed.

"We saw a lot of whales, and got close to some, but never close enough. That's the thing about working with whales. You can't tell them what to do. All you can do is get into the water and see what happens."

What happened took Westerskov by surprise. "I was floating at the surface, staring into the deep blue nothingness of the ocean. Suddenly a white shape appeared in the distance. It grew steadily larger. It was a baby humpback, about five metres long and probably weighing a couple of tonnes. First it swam past me, almost touching me with one of its pectoral fins. Then it turned and, very deliberately, caught me with its fin and carried me along for a short distance. I was looking straight into its eye, less than a metre away.

"Soon it released me. Then its mother appeared out of the depths, and I watched the two of them glide away out of sight. It all happened in a couple of minutes."

Westerskov's first reaction was to wonder whether he had captured the final moments on film. Or, in the excitement of such a rare event, had he simply forgotten to press the shutter?

When the films were processed, sure enough, there was the whale. That two-minute encounter made up for an otherwise frustrating four weeks.

While few *New Zealand Geographic* freelancers have had the chance to hobnob with humpbacks, Westerskov is not the only one to have returned from an assignment with an unusual tale.

Writer Mark Scott is one of those people who seem to find drama at every turn. Scott, with his two young daughters on board, had driven a jetboat up the Waikato River to near the floodgates of one of the river's hydroelectricity dams. When it was time to leave, the motor wouldn't start. It was winter, and raining. There wasn't a soul around. And within minutes the floodgates would be opened, sending a torrent of water down the gorge.

Scott describes the event: "I had worn out the battery trying to start the boat. While I was waiting for it to recover, I heard the chug of a diesel engine through the gathering gloom. Between squalls I could make out the shape of a tractor mowing the far end of the river

Adventurers all. New Zealand Geographic *contributors on assignment include (clockwise from far left) Charles Lindsay looping the loop in a Tiger Moth, Raewyn Mackenzie meeting a sea lion, John Walsby examining fossil-bearing rocks, Arno Gasteiger on an island owned by a hermit, Vaughan Yarwood and son Theo watching an eye operation on a lion, Warren Judd extracting a giant land snail from a rotting log, Dave Gunson working on a set of dinosaur paintings, Michael Schneider photographing glow-worms, Mark Scott in Bosnia and Kim Westerskov at -50°C in Antarctica.*

reserve. But the surge of relief I felt at this saviour in bright yellow raingear—for some inexplicable reason arriving at just this moment and in this weather—was way premature.

"Safe from prying eyes—so he thought—the mower man was working his machine with a certain flourish, turning his mundane chore into some mini-Grand Prix event. While I hollered and waved towels with real desperation, he was lost in his own exacting world of precision mowing.

"I waved. He pirouetted at the end of each run, the lighter front wheels of his machine satisfyingly skittering across the grass in a controlled slide. I hollered. He was zooming between the trees as though they were the markers in a Monte Carlo chicane. My children waved. He was busy hoisting the mowing gear between runs so that not a second was wasted mowing a single blade of previously-cut grass.

"Not once did this anonymous Denny Hulme astride his Massey Ferguson look up from his job. But who could blame him for extracting some interest from his task, or for that matter, in the freezing cold and wet, wanting to get home? It was a desire earnestly shared aboard our boat."

Though Scott admitted that he indulged a secret hankering to ride the roaring maelstrom, the outboard finally kicked in, and he was able to scuttle downriver to safety.

Safety was a weightier concern when Scott was in Bosnia in mid-1995, researching an article on the New Zealand peacekeeping contingent. Staring down the barrel of a Serbian tank only a few hundred metres away aroused sober thoughts of life's transience.

Arno Gasteiger, an Austrian-born photographer whose work has appeared in almost every issue of the magazine, had similar thoughts during a flight in a microlight over kauri forest.

The pilot's preamble did nothing to inspire confidence, recalled Gasteiger. "He told me he hadn't flown for a year since his brother crashed and died. Then he told me there was a storm coming, but since I was there already we might as well go up.

"'Don't go up on my account,' I told him. 'I can wait for a better day.'

"The guy insisted that we should go, and asked me to help him chase some bulls off the airstrip so we could take off.

"'Don't usually fly over bush,' he yelled at me when we were up. 'These things have a habit of stopping in mid-air.'

"By this stage I was thinking about my life insurance. The wind had come up and the pilot was gripping the stick and weaving around like a madman. I've never thanked any pilot more than I thanked him when we landed."

Living on islands as we do, many *New Zealand Geographic* stories have necessitated voyages by sea. And for many of our contributors, *mal de mer* has struck with a vengeance. Writer Raewyn Mackenzie, travelling aboard a fishing boat to Campbell Island for an article in the first issue (pages 184-191), took the precaution of taking anti-nausea tablets. While the medication contained her queasiness, it had the unpleasant side-effect of causing blurred vision and giddiness. She conducted eight interviews in a row, "oblivious to whether my brain was connecting with my hand."

BOB MARTIN

A 1993 New Zealand Geographic *poster on edible fungi was illustrated with cartoon-style figures depicting 16 species. The common puffball, often found on golf courses, lawns and parks, is tasty crumbed and served with tamarillo sauce, readers were informed.*

COLIN EDGERLEY

To accompany a feature on the Whanganui River in 1989, artist Colin Edgerley was commissioned to depict the river's rich history in poster form. His artwork included poet James K. Baxter and Mother Mary Aubert, a champion of the poor, along with paddle steamers which plied the "Rhine of New Zealand" during the early 1900s, and carved Maori poles.

COLIN EDGERLEY

The bird-eat-bird world of early New Zealand was the subject of an illustration for a 1989 article on the extinct Harpagornis eagle. Artist Edgerley depicted the eagle attacking a flightless moa—another extinct New Zealand bird.

Warren Judd sailed through his first assignment for the magazine—a story on deep sea fishing—with stomach intact, but claimed that the experience cured him of any interest in catching fish. "Once you've seen your first tonne of orange roughy landed, the next two hundred hold little fascination. The whole business completely loses its charm." Watching mountains of the bright red fish being dumped on the deck in front of him, to then slither in a pulpy mass below decks, also cured his appetite, he says.

Judd couldn't have completely lost interest in piscatorial pursuits, because he later covered the country's largest fishing contest, the Ninety Mile Beach Snapper Classic. As well, his wide-ranging interests have led him to write about school science fairs, antique furniture and oil wells. The story dearest to his heart, however, was the one he wrote on New Zealand's giant carnivorous land snails. These creatures, though impressive in size, are extremely reticent. Judd and photographer Michael Schneider, having succeeded in finding three or four live specimens embedded in the leaf litter of the forest floor, waited in vain for hours for them to emerge from their shells.

Judd, an expert on molluscs, decided to tempt the unwilling subjects with a meal of earth-worms—supposedly a favourite item of their diet. After scrabbling around in the freezing soil for close to an hour—it was the middle of winter—he came up with three puny specimens, and carefully placed them near the openings of the snail shells. Photographer Schneider resumed his vigil, camera poised.

Thirty minutes later, the snails still hadn't emerged when a bush robin swooped down from the trees and snaffled the worms.

Judd failed to find any replacements, and the pair left on nightfall without pictures.

Patience in the face of obstinate wildlife is something Michael Schneider has needed in hefty doses over the years. Schneider has been assigned to cover spiders, bats, glow-worms, tuatara, kea, bees (two types), snails and weta. He has kept a hive of honeybees in his bed-room so that he could photograph their activities at all hours, and on one occasion stood for four hours on a ladder waiting for bats to emerge from a hole in a tree roost. "I even had my dinner up the ladder," he says.

Many of his assignments have taken him to remote wildlife sanctuaries where the diversity of animal life is astonishing. He particularly enjoys working in these places at night.

"The forest is so full of noise and activity," he says. "You get used to things dropping on to your head and crawling over your face, or crashing into your headlamp. You don't realise how many creatures are out there. And you have to watch your step constantly or you're likely to squash something. Strangely enough, I feel safer in the bush at night than I do walking around the city."

For Schneider, the chance to work alongside conservation scientists has been a satisfying bonus to the job of taking photographs. "They're amazingly focused, dedicated people," he says. "Watching them work, helping them put bands on birds or radio transmitters on bats, or carry tuatara eggs that will one day help repopulate island reserves—you get caught up in it all, and it lifts your own level of motivation."

The cover of the first issue showed a black-browed mollymawk and chick on Campbell Island—a nature refuge 600 km south of New Zealand. Another bird which featured in the premier issue was "Old Blue," a black robin which survived and bred for double the usual black robin lifespan, and effectively saved her species from extinction. She became an unofficial emblem of New Zealand Geographic during its early years. The painting was by Vivian Ward.

BRIAN DONOVAN

As well as contributing astrophotographs for New Zealand Geographic's *regular space column, Brian Donovan supplied this innovative image of the path taken by the Sun during a day, photographed in a single exposure.*

Often the biggest battle photographers face is the weather. Murphy's Law of Photography states that when you need fine weather it will be raining, when you need wet weather it will be blazing, and when conditions are perfect there'll be no film in the camera. Despatched to photograph the newly opened Kepler Track, Dennis Brett phoned after a week to say that the track was completely under water. We feared the worst (not for Dennis, it has to be admitted, but for the assignment). We needn't have. The saturated landscape yielded pictures that perfectly captured the essence of Fiordland.

On assignment, the unexpected is always just around the corner. *Geographic* contributors have been mistaken for undercover police officers, drug dealers and even a fisheries spy. One was attacked by a cameraman at a New Year's Eve party in Antarctica; another by a sea lion in the Auckland Islands.

The mark of a good freelancer is a willingness to get personally involved in the story. But where do you draw the line? This was a question writer Vaughan Yarwood had to face during his research on the remote Chatham Islands, to the east of the mainland. Yarwood, who has written for the magazine on kauri (pages 62-71), zoos, dinosaurs and other subjects, had spent a day with a fishing family talking over the problems of the despised fish quota system, which locals say deprives the islands of revenue that is rightfully theirs.

As evening fell, his host asked in a tentative way whether he had ever tasted albatross. Yarwood knew that the big, handsome birds, once taken by Moriori in high-risk hunting expeditions to outlying islands, were regarded as a delicacy, and, though protected by law, still found their way into local ovens. The defiantly independent islanders admit as much, calling the birds "illegal Tegel" after a brand of frozen poultry.

"I confessed I had never taken a knife and fork to one," said Yarwood. "With the flourish of someone lifting a cherished wine from the cellar, my host hauled a plucked albatross from the freezer and set about preparing it for the table. It had been 'found dead,' I was told, and with the ritual of denial over, we began the meal.

"I expected an exquisite taste of the forbidden; the sort of delicate caress of the palate you might expect from a unicorn steak. I should have known better. The albatross flesh tasted somewhere between pullet and pilchard. I had risked my mariner's soul for a fish-fed fowl. But I had also, I later realised, cast a vote for the islanders and against Big Brother. I had become implicated."

While writing about another island—Great Barrier—Yarwood encountered a bird of an entirely different feather. At that time, an amphibian service operated from Auckland to the Barrier, using Widgeons. On the return trip, as the plane taxied out of the bay, a wing clipped a pohutukawa branch, causing the aircraft to twist sideways and drift into the tree. Said Yarwood: "The pilot stopped the engines, took off his shoes and socks and climbed on to the wing to push the aircraft into open water. He clambered back inside, murmured, 'Seems to be all right,' and we flew off. For him, surprises held no sting—I liked that."

New Zealand and its dependencies span latitudes from near the Equator to the South Pole. Nearest landmass to the west is Australia; to the east, South America.

DAVE GUNSON

Common spiders of home and garden are just one of many subjects Dave Gunson has illustrated for the magazine. Dinosaurs, deep water fish, bumblebees, possums and clouds have also been rendered by the Gunson palette.

The world in miniature

GEOFF MASON

Remote Raukumara Range forms a dramatic backdrop for 54 Maori retracing historic forest trails during a journey across East Cape in 1993. Strong connections with ancestral lands are at the heart of Maoridom.

"Tropic light, jungle luxuriance, the snow of Switzerland, the safety of England—here they all are at once." So wrote a tourist in the 1920s after visiting Milford Track, touted at that time as "the finest walk in the world."

The traveller might well have added "the beaches of Queensland, the sun of Majorca and the soil of Kentucky" to his list, for glowing comparisons are the visitor's stock reaction to this land; this world in miniature.

In an aircraft, you can pass over steaming volcanic cauldrons of mud and sulphur in the central North Island, and half an hour later be staring at an endless vista of snowcapped alps and mighty rivers of ice in the South. Within minutes, the terrain changes again to a patchwork counterpane of dead-flat fields, torn by braided rivers that flush snow-melt to the sea.

Even a modest car journey through Northland will take you through forests of giant kauri, many of them over a thousand years old, past wet glades of lichen-draped mangroves, echoing to the gunshot retorts of snapping shrimp, across acre after rolling acre of farmland, beside sand dunes so glittering white that you can hardly look at them.

Such diversity packed into one small country is one of the abiding impressions of the visitor. For residents, however—particularly those of colonial stock—the geographical nuances have often been ignored, subordinated by the work ethic and the quest for productivity that were founding principles of the nation.

To European settlers, majestic rainforest was merely "bush" to be cleared or "timber" to be felled; fair rolling hills merely good "country" to be brought in for grazing. Wetlands were waste lands to be drained and reclaimed. The settler's tools were an axe, a match and a bag of grass seed; his business was to create "the Britain of the South Pacific."

Today's citizen of Aotearoa is more likely to celebrate the Pacificness of a country that can never, finally, be a suburb of Europe. With its northern tip pointing to the tropics like a finger and its southern ramparts looking Antarctica square in the face, New Zealand's placement on the globe is starting to mean more to us than our historical attachments to Queen

GARETH EYRES

Like a giant footprint, eroded sandy pinnacles stand out against the arid pastures of Mesopotamia Station, the Canterbury sheep run owned by Samuel Butler. The novel Erewhon *drew on his experiences in New Zealand.*

DEREK GRZELEWSKI

Caught by an early winter storm, a tramper passes through beech forest on the Routeburn Track—the country's most popular alpine walk. For six months of the year, the track is snowbound and often impassable.

and Commonwealth.

And with this change in consciousness is the realisation that the colonial legacy of indifference and outright cruelty to the land is overdue for change.

The tangata whenua—the people of the land—have some important lessons to teach us on this subject. Respect, for one thing. Maori were more likely to give a venerable tree a name than to calculate how many woolsheds could be built from its timber. No South Island Maori climber would lift his head above the summit of Mt Cook (Aoraki—"cloud piercer"); to do so would be to insult the noble peak. To minds shaped by Western influence, such attitudes may seem anachronistic, irrelevant even.

But there is a deeper truth here. It is the difference between possessing land and being possessed by land. It is learning to see beyond the quick gains of exploitation to the need for a long-term balance between people and planet. If it takes personification of the sea as Tangaroa to curb human greed for fish, or the forest as Tane to halt the destruction of tree and tree-dweller, surely that is better than apologising to future generations for leaving them empty oceans and bland hills.

In Maori legend, land and sky, Papatuanuku and Rangitane, are star-crossed lovers: forever linked; forever separate. Rangi waters Papa with his tears of longing; Papa's children, the forests and creatures, reach up to their father. This kind of connectedness offers a starting point for the modern quest for a "sense of place." And it permeates the writing and photography of the land which *New Zealand Geographic* has tried to foster. Not the land as a commodity to be seen, snapped, then ticked off the traveller's itinerary, but the land as part of the lives of those who walk upon it, draw sustenance from it, own it and are owned by it.

A rejection of the commodity approach to land leads inevitably to a rejection of "pin-up" landscape photographs that have more to do with selling than with seeing. The style of photography we try to achieve combines the passion of the artist with the curiosity of the scientist—and the patience of the hermit! We want images that are both direct and natural—not artificially sweetened by tricks of camera and film—and which reward the spirit.

The best pictures seem to grow out of the land itself, and somehow transfuse themselves into celluloid. They arise when the photographer manages to do what Eugene Smith, the father of photojournalism, called "snaring truth in a web of light."

Only that which is made with time will be remembered in time, said Rodin. Of course, we want our pictures to be remembered. Not to elicit a superficial "wow"—a visual snort of colour and form that appeals for an instant before the page is turned—but a deeper response that resonates in the reader's mind like a gong.

"I did see the mists and the clouds and the rain covering and uncovering the primeval. I did know heartache at wilderness beauty," wrote New Zealand novelist John A. Lee of the hinterland. Some measure of heartache—a mixture of gratitude for what remains and regret for what has gone—is a prerequisite if we are to find our place in the world as something more than a jewel box of geographical gems.

It is the goal worthy of the land we call home.

ARNO GASTEIGER

Golden Bay, hidden among mountains in the north-west corner of the South Island, is limestone and marble country. One of many impressive caverns chiselled out of the earth is Rawhiti Cave, an estimated million years old.

preceding pages: ANDRIS APSE

Water, rock and forest are the essential elements of Fiordland National Park—at over 1.2 million hectares, New Zealand's largest wilderness park. Island-studded Lake Manapouri is flanked by the Kepler Mountains beyond.

DARRYL TORCKLER

An underwater forest of mosses, liverworts, water forget-me-nots and cress greets divers in New Zealand's largest and clearest freshwater springs: Pupu Springs. The visibility is over 60 metres; the temperature a constant 11.7°C.

DEREK GRZELEWSKI

*The mountainous spine of the South Island—the Southern Alps—has long been a magnet to climbers. The jewel in
the crown is Aoraki, Mt Cook, here beckoning in pre-dawn light as a party prepares for an ascent.*

ARNO GASTEIGER

Golden at sunset, the town of Bluff is synonymous with oysters dredged from nearby Foveaux Strait. In recent years, gourmets have had to do without the king of shellfish: dwindling stocks have seen the beds closed to harvesting.

ARNO GASTEIGER

Sheep farming no longer has the economic centrality it once boasted, but there is no doubting that New Zealand is still a land of wool and lamb. Even on remote islands like d'Urville, an outpost of the Marlborough Sounds, sheep are a way of life.

MILES WISLANG

Melting at the terminus of New Zealand's largest river of ice—the 27-kilometre-long Tasman Glacier—results in dramatic but short-lived structures such as this ice bridge. Ice in the glacier reaches 600 metres in thickness.

ARNO GASTEIGER

*Spectacular thermal areas show the country to be part of the Pacific Ring of Fire, a volcanically volatile portion of
the Earth's crust. Hot mineral-rich water exits Champagne Pool, one of many thermal attractions in Rotorua.*

following pages: ARNO GASTEIGER

*Although more than 80 per cent of the New Zealand population now resides in towns and cities, it is rural scenes
such as this one, overlooking Golden Bay, which remain the dominant geographic "signature" of the country.*

Kauri

By VAUGHAN YARWOOD

Abridged from New Zealand Geographic, *April - June, 1989*

THE MASSIVE PILLARS rise out of the hillside as though they have always been there, surrounded by a reckless litter of leaf and bark; as though their powerful boughs, draped with hanging plants, have always held the sky away from the land.

In the silence of the valley every sound is distinct—a jagged birdcall, the fall to earth of a golden branch, the muffled hiss of river water.

I am in Northland's Waima Forest, somewhere above the Waiotemarama Stream, in a stand of kauri stretching away up the ridge in tiers. Underpinned with kauri grass, tree ferns and ribbed spears of lancewood, they dominate the landscape, giving the impression that there is a lesser forest growing beneath the ruins of some otherworldly architecture.

Looking directly up towards the crown, the oyster-flaked trunks ripple and twist with pent-up strength. Their sheer size seems to scorn the natural forces which play havoc with other living things.

Shakespeare's lines about Julius Caesar "bestriding the narrow world like a Colossus" seem made for the kauri. But, like Caesar, most of the forest giants have fallen, victims of the sudden blade, since the human colonisation of New Zealand.

A tragic mix of ignorance, greed and necessity decimated their numbers within a single lifetime. Now pockets lie scattered in the least accessible parts of Northland's ranges and across open farm-land—remnants of the vast rainforests which grew north of a line stretching from Kawhia to Tauranga.

The early Maori, struck by the kauri's imposing stature, told how the whale once wanted the huge tree to live in the ocean as a brother, but, failing to persuade him, managed to swap skins. Which is why, they said, the kauri's bark is so thin and full of resin.

Maori quickly found uses for the tree, which ranked second in importance only to totara, with its regal red timber. Kauri gum torches were made for night fishing, gum smoke used as an insect repellent and soot as the pigment in intricately tattooed moko. Softened by soaking in water and mixed with the milk of the puha, the honey-coloured gum even became an aromatic chewing gum.

IAN MACDONALD

Dawn mists bathe stands of kauri—the king of New Zealand trees—in Puketi, one of Northland's forest sanctuaries.

Where the durable totara was not available, northern tribes felled and hollowed out suitable kauri for their canoes, some of which reached 20 or more metres in length.

The first European description of the trees came when Frenchman Marion du Fresne sailed into the Bay of Islands for repairs in 1772. "The tree which prevails most of all in the

Ramrod-straight, young kauri trees called rickers rise out of swards of kauri grass in Waipoua Forest. A mature tree in nearby Puketi Forest (opposite) may be over a thousand years old.

forests is the olive-leafed cedar," wrote his second in command, Crozet. "Its wood is elastic and I judged it very suitable for making ships' masts." The French set about felling two trees, but local Maori turned against them; du Fresne and 25 others were killed, and the unfinished spars were abandoned.

However, the light, straight-grained "cowrie" soon proved itself unrivalled on board ship and became indispensable to the British navy. The story persists that Nelson's flagship at the battle of Trafalgar carried New Zealand kauri aloft.

Young trees (rickers) suitable for spars were not common

on the coast, so attention turned to the vast inland forests. A team of bullocks—giant pakeha "dogs" to the Maori—was brought over from Australia to make the job of extracting felled trees less arduous. These docile and intelligent animals were to become a powerhouse of the kauri harvest in future years.

Gumdigging, and later the bleeding of living trees, progressed hand in hand with the felling of kauri, and gum became a major export. Unscrupulous diggers caused great damage through illegal burn-offs and excessive bleeding, which often amounted to ringbarking.

By the time Auckland became the country's capital in 1840, kauri planking was being exported, and coastal mills were cutting on both shores of Northland.

Auckland became a pump, sucking timber from the carcass of the land. Cut in increasingly remote regions and flushed down rivers and tributaries through a network of driving dams, the logs were collected by coastal booms. Here they were either milled on site, trimmed for shipping overseas or lashed together herringbone-fashion and towed to Auckland.

As early as 1861, nine out of ten houses built in the city were made of kauri. And not just the weatherboards. They could almost have been hollowed out of the sweetly scented trees, for the quantities each building consumed. Ceilings, wall linings, shingles, doors, skirtings, furniture, butter churns, mantelpieces—almost any domestic item could be, and was, manufactured from borer-resistant heart kauri.

The Otamatea Kauri and Pioneer Museum overlooks the upper reaches of the Kaipara Harbour, a body of water which, in its heyday, was jammed with ships loading kauri. The museum's director, Merv Sterling, one-time gumdigger and elder statesman of kauri lore, has presided over the assembly of an extraordinary range of kauri relics, including the gear used to extract logs from the bush.

"Kauri varnish is the best in the world for musical instruments," he says, delighted to dwell on some of the tree's lesser-known uses. "The gum was used for lacquers, paint and linoleum. In India they used it to make impressions for false teeth."

Not unnaturally, for someone who has salvaged so much of the kauri's past, his chief concern is with the tree's continuing disappearance from the land.

"All the trees around here have gone in the last three years—some quite big ones, too. One of the biggest enemies of the remaining stands is the boatbuilders. Anyone who can afford a boat worth a quarter of a million dollars isn't too concerned about the price tag on the timber—it's as simple as that."

John Diamond, an historian who has lived and breathed kauri for much of his life, lives on the fringe of the Waitakere Ranges, at one time Auckland's nearest source of kauri. He has

interviewed many bushmen, the oldest born in 1864. In the mid-1920s, when the local kauri industry was still alive, he often pushbiked out to Bethells Beach, west of Auckland, stopping off at the small mills with their networks of tramlines, steam engines and half a dozen men.

"Bushmen liked the bush, but they still cut it down," he says. "It was their job. They knew it would all be exhausted, just as we know oil will run out." He says Auckland's lack of building stone and patchy clay deposits for brickworks made kauri the natural choice for construction. But the waste of timber was colossal. Prime heart kauri was shipped across the Tasman as paving for Melbourne streets; thousands of tonnes were consumed in the construction of driving dams, and many

An eerie landscape of destruction shows how thoroughly the forest was stripped in some areas. Only the trunks were taken, leaving massive amounts of timber in the crowns to rot.

Alexander Turnbull Library photograph

thousands more were pulverised on their way downstream. Incalculable quantities were left to rot in the forest as sap and crown timber because only the clean trunks were valued.

Some of the drives, for which logs had been stockpiled for many years, held up to 10,000 logs and several flushes were needed to clear the river. The frequent jams were either jacked free or broken up with dynamite.

Of the total volume of kauri growing in the north before logging began, it has been estimated that less than half was brought to market.

In the last decades of the twentieth century, everything has been stood on its head. Loggers can call on sophisticated machinery, and are restrained by a consideration for the environment which, even 50 years ago, would have been inexplicable.

But now there is little timber. For the next one, two, or even three hundred years kauri is destined to follow the life of royalty: to be talked about, vigorously protected, much loved and rarely seen.

Northland Kauri, run by the Bergman brothers of Pakaraka, is one of a handful of companies still felling kauri. Manager Chris Bergman is disappointed I hadn't arrived a few weeks earlier. "We cut out a stand on private land in Hikurangi. Three good-sized trees and half a dozen small ones," he says. "The biggest was two metres wide."

Bergman uses Alaskan milling techniques, flying in a lightweight chainsaw mill, making camp and slabbing the timber up in the bush before flying it out. The technique, he says, causes no more damage than a falling kauri would. "We don't have to push roads in, and all we leave is sawdust—and a cheque—$25,000 to the Hikurangi farmer."

Much of the demand for kauri is fuelled by boatbuilders, and they come to timber yards with full wallets. Why do they esteem kauri so highly?

Although the wood has a number of good general properties (straight grain, no knots, light, strong, superb finishing qualities, available in long lengths and a heart wood resistant to borer) the thing that really sets it apart for boats is its behaviour when wet: kauri doesn't swell, shrink or distort. Only teak and one or two other hardwoods share this property, but they are much more difficult to work.

Ashby's boatyard, nestled in the Bay of Islands port of Opua, is a typical user of kauri. Every three years or so Jim Ashby clears a shed and lays the keel of a yacht which is far from run-of-the-mill. Special project at the moment is a 46-foot, 14-tonne cutter, built from laminated kauri.

Traditionally, he says, boats had single skins, but the bonded triple skins are lighter and stronger. "A boat like this is an art form today," says Jim. "In the past no one bothered about looks, but these days people like to see kauri, so we make a feature of it." Although $30,000-worth of timber will have gone into it when finished, this represents perhaps six per cent of the total cost. In other words, kauri has by no means priced itself off that luxury market.

One Auckland company is tackling the problem of supply from a different angle: recycling the product of past forest destruction. Sixty per cent of the Kauri Timber Company's business is kauri retrieved from the demolition of old buildings.

"There are big volumes out there at the moment," says manager Barry Brown. "It will drop again, but over the last few years supply has been fairly constant."

GEOFF OSBORNE

Renall Street, Ponsonby, preserves the appearance of 19th century Auckland, when nine out of ten houses were built of kauri. Straight-grained, resistant to borer and readily available, kauri was a builder's dream. Today, only the wealthy can afford the timber, which has become a rarity.

GEOFF OSBORNE

Polish-born carver Mirek
Sulkowski salutes a bygone era
with four kauri busts. Clockwise
from top left: Tudor Collins,
kauri bushman and photo-
grapher; Sir A. H. Reed,

publisher, writer and historian;
Gordon Coates, first New
Zealand-born prime minister;
Prof. W. R. McGregor, central
figure in the fight to save
Waipoua Forest.

He says boatbuilders, who use only the highest grade of straight-grained kauri because of its strength, are now turning to sap kauri. Long dismissed because of its susceptibility to decay, it can be used after tanalising, although the green colour is a disadvantage. Heart kauri, with its attractive silvery fleck, is still preferred.

"Heart kauri planking," says fourth generation sawmiller Stephen Lane of Lane and Sons, Totara North, "is sound for at least 100 years." He is in a good position to know, as his family business built scores of ships of up to 350 tonnes between 1870 and 1910.

"In the United States, kauri has always been recognised as the premium timber for wooden boats." Lane continues, "We can't get enough good [heart] timber to meet the boatbuilding demand."

Barry Brown and Chris Bergman both believe that giving access to dead trees in the former state forests would greatly help the supply of kauri. Says Brown, "There are colossal volumes of dead trees—I've seen 80 dead trees in Warawara Forest which could be taken for a start."

Controlled extraction could mean an end to the felling of green trees on private land.

Stephen Lane is less convinced. "You can't be as certain of the strength and quality of dead wood—it may have already been sitting there for a hundred years. If you were going to pay a million dollars for a high class yacht, and your life might depend on its strength, would you like me to substitute unproven wood?"

He would prefer to see a resumption of the selective logging his company carried out prior to 1980.

"Puketi contains 7000 hectares of kauri, and in 10 years we removed only a quarter of the larger trees from 100 hectares. A large tree provides 20-30 cubic metres of wood, and taking 10 large trees a year would provide sufficient kauri to undergird a $25 million-a-year luxury boatbuilding trade with the US. Shutting up forests in perpetuity will lead to trees becoming over-mature. They will die and their timber will be wasted."

Botanists have long noted that mature kauri stands contain few young trees and seedlings to repopulate the forest once the giants die. Lack of light under big trees, a harsh, acid leaf litter and a ransacked clay soil prevent seedlings flourishing. So how has the species perpetuated itself over the last 60 million years?

John Ogden, a forest ecologist at Auckland University, argues that the trees live so long that eventually some natural disaster (fire, cyclone, volcano) will devastate a section of mature forest. A quick-growing "nurse crop" such as manuka will colonise this decimated area, and then all it takes is one or two remaining kauri or some residual viable seed to spawn a new generation of young trees.

Maximum growth in a kauri forest occurs at an adolescent (for kauri) 160 years of age, and maturity approaches at about 600 years. Most trees of over 1000 years deteriorate. The hearts rot out to leave giant living pipes, and the crowns atrophy—as can be seen in most of the big, over-mature trees today.

Professor Tim Whitmore of Oxford University, an internationally recognised expert on all *Agathis* species, went so far as to describe Waipoua Forest as a "deteriorating grove of moribund old kauri" in urgent need of a big shake-out!

Such an event occurred in 1959, when a hurricane toppled an estimated 10 per cent of large kauri in Puketi and damaged many others in nearby forests as well. It is this sort of wastage that some loggers and forest managers seek to pre-empt by selective logging.

Such techniques, however, are anathema to conservation groups, who vehemently oppose any sort of logging in native forests. They hold that kauri require so long to reach giant proportions that they really do represent a non-renewable resource.

Debate over the management of kauri forests is nothing new. Waipoua, now the country's largest kauri remnant, was originally gazetted as "waste lands" when it was purchased from the Maori in 1876. In 1913 a Royal Commission on Forestry reported that its 9100 hectares was too large for a reserve, and could comfortably be reduced to 80 hectares. Following logging, the report noted, most of the land could be settled.

It is daunting to realise that the rainforest which nurtured giants like Tane Mahuta and Te Matua Ngahere, and which now attracts upwards of 60,000 visitors a year, was credited with no intrinsic value whatsoever.

Yet the forest survived both the recommendations and a state highway cut through in 1928. In the 1940s, however, selective logging was introduced into Waipoua in the guise of providing "essential war materials." The move caused widespread unease.

Professor Barney McGregor, a zoologist at the University of Auckland, wrote: "Nature does many things only once. Only once did she make a kauri forest, and this was one of the most sublime of all her noble works. By chance the kauri forests were entrusted to our care. We have destroyed them almost completely, all but this last and pitiful remnant."

He described Waipoua as: "A remnant of an incredibly ancient garden . . . set in the midst of a vast dim-aisled cathedral that entombs an eternal silence."

Public opinion eventually triumphed over bureaucracy, and in 1952 Waipoua was proclaimed a forest sanctuary.

A similar outcry saw selective logging in Warawara end dramatically in 1974, although it was not until March 1985 that the chainsaws finally quit state kauri forests altogether.

Ironically, in safeguarding the remaining publicly-owned kauri, conservationists may have shot themselves in the foot. With demand for the timber unchecked, and prices high, felling on private land has rocketed. Choice trees that even the millers concede should be preserved are being felled.

A second repercussion is Pacific-wide. Fijian kauri, its timber almost indistinguishable from New Zealand's *Agathis australis,* is being milled to fill the vacuum. Says John Halkett, a Forest Service principal forester now with the Department of Conservation, "Compared with New Zealand's efforts, logging in Fiji is a rape and pillage affair. Some logged areas look like the other side of the moon. We have exported our supply problem and are hastening the extermination of someone else's forest instead of our own."

The depletion of Fiji's forests highlights the neglect of native silvicultural research in New Zealand. Given the questions surrounding our use of substitute tropical timber, and the prohibition on extraction of kauri from DOC-administered forests, the only responsible supply long-term would seem to be from commercial plantations.

Surprisingly, none exist.

However, there are large areas of regenerating kauri. The

ARNO GASTEIGER

All conifers produce resins, but kauri is one of the most prodigious bleeders. As the glutinous resin seeps out of the tree, it can trap insects, entombing them for all time in a golden coffin.

burning and slaughter perpetrated by our forebears has, ironically, reinitiated the forests. Correctly managed, such forests could become a valuable and renewable source of timber.

In the 1950s research was begun to find out how growth rates of young trees could be improved by management practices such as various levels of thinning and fertiliser application. The results were striking. Whereas crowded trees put on a centimetre in diameter every 8-10 years, thinned trees achieved the same growth in a single year.

However, since the state forests were "locked up," even this research has shrivelled. Perhaps there is a fear that any successfully managed forest may end up being "sanctified"—and foresters don't seem interested in producing tree museums.

Even well-managed kauri are unlikely to be ready for harvest in less than 80-120 years, compared with radiata pine's 28 years. Yet Graeme Platt, a nurseryman specialising in the raising of native plants, is adamant the potential of kauri as a commercial timber has not been fully understood.

"*Pinus radiata* has spoilt us," he says. "The kauri's yield of millable timber per year of growth is quite respectable—up to 10 m³/ha/yr. But in New Zealand we haven't learned to assign forests a standing value as they have in Europe. Northern Hemisphere forests are thought of as an investment to be enjoyed by future generations. We work with pine, a tree which reaches maturity in a single lifetime. That sort of harvest mentality has to go before kauri can be seen to be commercially viable."

The kauri forests may now be safe from logging, but other threats remain. Possums are a major problem, not for kauri directly but for sister trees such as rata, which they are chewing to death. More than 50 per cent of the rata in Puketi are already dead, and the possums are spreading north.

All is not gloom, however, for McGregor's "vast dim-aisled cathedrals." From the ceaseless rasp of saws and nick of bleeders' knives, from the very ashes of the kauri past, a phoenix is about to rise. A national park embracing all Crown kauri forests north of Auckland is edging towards birth.

In total, 92,000 hectares, including important non-kauri natural features such as the Kai Iwi Lakes, towering Maunganui Bluff and impressive Kahakaroa, Hokianga Harbour's big dune, have been earmarked for inclusion. Until now there has been no subtropical equivalent of the subantarctic zones represented by beech and podocarp forests in southern National Parks.

Much of the land under discussion is subject to Maori land claims—a process to which the Northland National Parks and Reserves Board is committed. Board member Tupi Puriri, himself paramount rangatira of Northland's Ngapuhi tribe, says individual Maori tribes are likely to support the park concept once their land claims are recognised. "It depends how the old people view things. If the Waitangi Tribunal rules in their favour I am confident they will want their land protected as part of the national park," he says.

Years ago, beyond the memory of most of us, destruction visited the northern rainforests like a plague, attracted by the incomparable riches of the kauri. How fitting if that same massive tree became through this new park the instrument of the forests' salvation . . .

As I leave the forest behind and edge into Auckland's evening traffic, the vision lingers of those hammered trunks, still holding the earth from the sky.

ARNO GASTEIGER

Pressure underground converts bland resin into golden gum. When polished, such pieces form poignant reminders of the fallen trees. In this lump, several resin flows have covered each other.

Wild coast

By GERARD HINDMARSH
Photographs by ANDREW DIXON

Abridged from New Zealand Geographic, *April - June, 1992*

TO ME IT WILL ALWAYS BE "the impassable coast"—that section of primeval coastline that stretches 30 km between the Heaphy River in the south and the Kahurangi in the north.

It has always attracted me; an area so harsh and inaccessible that it has remained virtually untouched. A wild place that deprives of comfort, replenishes the soul and reminds us what this country once looked like. Protected by the vast hinterland of North West Nelson Forest Park, it remains the last section of true wilderness coast left outside of Fiordland and Stewart Island.

Before setting out, I talked to a few locals who had traversed the route and pored over maps and historical notes—in particular Charles Heaphy's account of his 1846 journey with Thomas Brunner from Massacre (Golden) Bay down the West Coast to Arahura and back—a five-month marathon.

They were the first Europeans to traverse this section of coast, and their journey created intense interest. William Fox, then the New Zealand Company agent at Nelson, wrote, "I think Messrs Brunner and Heaphy are entitled to the credit of having accomplished the most arduous expedition which has yet been undertaken in New Zealand."

I began to imagine a trip that followed in the footsteps—and handholds—of these intrepid explorers. As ambition ripened into obsession, I persuaded three others to join me: John Mitchell, Andrew Dixon and Brian Cooper. We planned to follow the coast from the Anatori River southwards to the Heaphy River where we could connect with the Heaphy Track to return.

After two months of training, we forded the Anatori River on Wednesday, November 20, 1991. The tide was high but ebbing as we made our way over giant blue papa rocks which had fallen from the Kaipuke Cliffs, and scrambled around bluffs between waves. This section of coast down to the Kahurangi River, referred to as the Taitapu Coast by Heaphy, affords relatively easy access with sandy beaches and low hills.

Where fences peter out under windblown dunes, cattle wander the beach. Near Kahurangi Point one remarkable dune intrudes right into the forest. I speculated whether or not Heaphy's descrip-

Clinging for dear life, the author edges around a wave-battered bluff near Kahurangi. A group of fur seals look on from their offshore haul-out.

tion of the "remarkable white landslip" at this point is the same dune we see today.

The epicentre of the 1929 Murchison earthquake was here, causing massive slumping into the sea and destroying the homes of lighthouse keepers. On June 17, Arthur Page and son Alva had been cutting scrub high above the house when they heard a terrific roar. The trees began to shake, and the men were thrown to their knees as the hillside heaved and cracked open.

As the land steadied, they ran back along the ridges to find a scene of devastation at home. A huge slip had crashed down on their house, smashing it against the lighthouse before flinging it over the cliff into the sea. From where they were standing it looked as if a 40-acre paddock had been floated out to sea, with cabbage trees and pongas still standing.

Despite their worst fears, they found Mrs Nellie Page unharmed; when the 'quake struck she had been climbing

"Like wading through a bowl of whipped cream" is how the author describes negotiating parts of the Kahurangi coast. "These waves could envelop you in a mantle of white, then throw you over as the underlying water hit you moments later."

through a fence. Terrified, she ran to keep just ahead of the widening slip as it crashed through her house with such force that it snapped knives and forks. Even though earth and debris built up six metres against the lighthouse, its solid concrete base and 25 mm cast iron construction saved it from serious damage.

Stricken by unfavourable weather from the start, Heaphy and Brunner were detained by heavy rain, and sought shelter in a cave after their throat-deep crossing of Big River. "Wet through during the whole of the day," wrote Heaphy in his

journal. The next day: "Rain and thick weather," followed by a day of "Strong S.W. gales and rain."

Heaphy describes the "curious but satisfactory meal" obtained by accompanying some local Maori on to the reefs. "The mutton fish, or pawa, although resembling india rubber in toughness and colour, is very excellent and substantial food for explorers, both European and native; and when it can be obtained, which is only at low water, spring tides, is much prized by those gentlemen. The sea urchin tastes like spider crab, and though very palatable, would be much improved by vinegar and condiments. But the sea anemone is the most *recherché*. Half animal, half vegetable, as we unscientific people must describe a zoophyte, it is the most extraordinary food that ever afforded nutriment to the human body, and must be eaten to be comprehended. Suffice to say that in its capture it must be jerked quickly from its holding on the rock, or it contracts itself into a small lump and nearly disappears in the crevice from which it grows. In cooking it, care should be taken to keep it apart from other victuals, and in eating it the eyes should be kept tightly shut."

Finally making camp at the Kahurangi River "from whence the difficulties of our path would commence," Heaphy and Brunner discussed the warning given to them by Eneho, an old Maori at Westhaven Inlet only days before: ". . . we should never reach Kawatiri, as any white man could not fail to be expended on the coast which lay near Rocky Point, and the old rascal and his companions grinned when he mentioned Tauparikaka cliff as the utmost possible limit of our journeying."

My companions and I received warnings of our own, from cattle musterers with whom we shared the relative comfort of the old lighthouse keeper's house at Kahurangi. "We had to rescue the last bloke that tried, and fell in," said one. "You'll be back this way Sunday. They all turn back," intoned another. It became a matter of considerable pride that we succeed. One recent attempt, recorded in the hut book, stated simply: "Karamea or Bust, and I Bust."

Next morning, after a hearty bacon-and-eggs breakfast washed down with left-over musterer's stew, we shouldered heavy packs and set off overland for the Kahurangi River, barely making headway as we strained forward into gale force winds. I thought again of Heaphy: "Our loads consisted of 35 lb of flour each, with tea, sugar, pearl barley, powder, shot, instruments, books, boots, two blankets, amounting to 80 lb each . . . being exceedingly fatiguing." I resolved not to complain of pack weight again.

At the Kahurangi River the geological formation of the country changes, and a coarse red granite appears, altering the character of the coast to precipitous cliffs and rugged offshore rocks. Heaphy was detained for a further two days here, constructing makeshift huts from nikau fronds. "At night the gale caused the water to rise so high as to break

South of Kahurangi Point, the heavily indented coastline, big surf and near-vertical cliffs present the coastal tramper with an abundance of challenges.

A razorback headland thrusting out into the Tasman forced the four travellers to abandon the coast and head up and over. The kiekie scrub, with its long spear- like leaves and thick stems, formed an almost impenetrable barrier. It had to be alternately walked over, crashed through and crawled under.

within a few feet of our huts, and to debar all passage along the beach; above us was a perpendicular cliff, and in front a swollen river, causing our situation to be at once unpleasant and exciting."

Squalls drove in from the south-west as we forded the river and boulder-hopped for only a few hundred metres before encountering a sheer bluff. Brian edged around on a high ledge before returning with the already suspected verdict: "Up and over!"

It would be no exaggeration to say that in some places it took 10 minutes to make 10 metres of progress, sweating and swearing up that almost vertical slope. Although the predominantly kiekie scrub afforded good holding, it had adapted well to the extreme coastal climate, forming an almost impenetrable interwoven barrier. We alternated between walking over it, crashing through it and crawling under it.

At the top we compared wounds and made reasonable progress through the rata and manuka before finding a steep slip to descend, only to realise at the bottom what a terrible mistake we had made. We were now sandwiched between the bluff we had just bypassed and another even worse, with the wind making even sitting difficult. The power of the waves hitting the cliffs below us was awesome. Their relentlessness confuses your equilibrium; sometimes you think you are clinging to a swaying cliff over a motionless sea. Add gale force wind, squally rain and the odd giant wave sending up spray that leaves you saturated, and you have one of Nature's headiest cocktails.

Having vowed only minutes before not to subject ourselves to any more "kiekie bashing," we retraced our steps back up the slip to the ridge, before finding a waterfall by which to descend to the coast once more.

The knowledge that we were walking into a natural storehouse gave us the confidence to expect to find our food en route. We took tea for the billy, but left behind the usual essentials in exchange for an old screwdriver (to prize off paua), knives and an onion sack to gather it all in.

John, who has a background in botany, would suggest what berries, plants or fungi might be edible, what seaweed would go well with the paua, or even what green wood could be relied on to burn when everything was wet. Brian was an eager hunter, knowing where to look for food by exercising a sensitivity to animal behaviour and the changing elements. Much of his boyhood had been spent clinging to cliffs in Yorkshire, searching out seabird eggs. Watching him climb ahead of me would often inspire a quizzical thought as to how he survived his childhood at all!

As the journey progressed, we also became expert in analysing wave patterns: watching for that extra-large recedence which would allow a headlong dash across a memorised series of boulders before the next wave surged in and covered the whole area in a sweeping breaker. Although

emergency procedures had been discussed, it became obvious that there would be little hope of rescue if one of us were swept out by a rogue wave. Heaphy himself describes waiting half an hour at one point "before a wave presented itself which we could deem safe."

We made good progress on the low tide rounding Otukoroiti Point to camp at Christabel Creek, having covered a bare four kilometres in just under eight hours. Unable to find sheltered campsites, we were forced to construct an enormous driftwood wall to stop our tent being blown away. We dined on paua, kina and sea lettuce as the red sun sank into the ocean. Surreptitiously flicking the seaweed off my plate, I noticed it landed next to two other small piles. "Nice sea lettuce, John," I said, grimacing.

We spent a restless night in gale force winds. John slept outside in an adjoining bay; he is simply at home in this sort of environment, and at least slept soundly without a flapping tent.

Seals became numerous as we traversed southward. We noticed that they sought out fresh water pools, and wondered if soaking in them was a way of ridding themselves of marine parasites. We often smelt them before we saw them, especially as we were usually walking into the wind. Sometimes the stench was overpowering. There are two smells that I shall always associate with this coast: firstly, the salt-laden smell that accompanies the incessant wind; secondly, the fetid smell of the seals.

Next day we pressed southwards again, over enormous house-sized rocks, each one a major obstacle. Several steep headlands dividing rocky bays necessitated scrambling up and over, often belaying with rope, before coming to Tauparikaka cliff.

The reader might casually enquire why we did not avail ourselves of an inland bypass whenever these obstacles blocked our progress. Heaphy's account at this point explains the predicament we were constantly faced with. "Against this projection the waves broke on the perpendicular face of the rock, so as completely to prevent it being passed below, while inshore the mountain rose steeply and high, presenting in that direction as impassable a barrier. About 80 feet above the sea, however, where the point jutted from the mountain, was a place which seemed as if it might afford footing along the summit: to this we ascended by a difficult rocky way, through karaka bushes and among large fragments of granite. On the other side the appearance of the way was appalling, and we certainly for a time deemed the descent impracticable without a ladder. The sight of a rotten native-made rope which dangled over the precipice made us perhaps imagine the descent to be more critical than it in reality was. At length, after looking down several times, we perceived a ledge and some holes in the face of the rock which might enable us to descend, and we summoned up courage to make the attempt.

The worst part of the way was round an overhanging rock, where it was necessary to lean backwards in order to get from one ledge to the other. Below this the way was less dangerous, but great care was yet necessary to avoid slipping from the slanting rock into the tide beneath."

We lunched at Seal Bay amid hundreds of seals—the first real colony. There were newborn pups everywhere, and the bulls were challenging each other for territory. The females, after coming ashore and giving birth to a single pup, mate again some ten days later. Unintentionally, we had chosen this rather intimate time for our intrusion, and had to be continually on our guard against hyperactive males and nervous females. We observed some ferocious fights: males tearing flesh from each other until they could barely move.

There was one anxious moment when Brian lurched sideways to avoid a lunging seal. In his haste he caught his boot between two boulders and sprained his ankle, collapsing in pain right beside the escaping seal. Andrew and I alternated between real concern and hoots of laughter as we helped him sit up. A few minutes' rest, and with the help of a stout stick, Brian was back up front with only a pronounced limp to hint that anything untoward had occurred.

Once a sealing station, this site had been abandoned some nine or ten years before Heaphy, on account of the depletion of seals. Small groups were noted by Heaphy, but did not appear to match today's abundance.

Beyond Seal Bay we came to a particularly obtuse bluff. The cliff rose vertically, but we had no alternative than to strike upwards as best we could, and hopefully cross into the mouth of the Moutere River. The few metres of loose, crumbly granite gravel, the transition zone between bare rock and scrubline, was often the most tortuous: no foot- or handhold could be trusted.

It was here that I experienced my most terrifying moments, inching upwards in toeholds I had cut with my Bowie knife, unable to even call out to Andrew for help because the words wouldn't come out. To finally grab the lowest flax and pull myself up through the steep kiekie was sweet relief indeed.

A wonderful view of the Moutere River, the first substantial watercourse since Kahurangi, provided a suitable excuse to rest on the small saddle. I felt physically drained, every exposed part of my skin was covered in kiekie cuts—deep incisions that seemed to get more painful by the hour—and I had become separated from the others.

I charged downwards, falling and stumbling through the kiekie before finding myself on the edge of a precipice with Brian below, shouting instructions on the best descent.

In fading light we chose a camp site just before Rocks Point under a beautiful nikau grove which provided good shelter from the continual wind and rain.

Next morning the wind was such that we had to lean forward and clutch rocks to pull ourselves around Rocks Point.

There before us was the luxurious sand stretch of Big Bay, with its majestic hills covered in nikau, rata, flax and kiekie, and creeks bubbling through gaps in the greenery.

The main seal colony at Wekakura Point required careful manoeuvring to get around. Newborn pups were everywhere, and the bulls were particularly aggressive, charging and bailing us up against the cliff.

We aborted an attempt to climb around this colony, wasting a good hour crawling upwards through steep flax before hitting totally impenetrable kiekie. Retracing our ascent and path back to a wonderful golden beach, we lit an enormous bonfire, and stood close around it in the rain, relishing the warmth on our damp bodies.

We used such times to rearrange or repair gear. The wear and tear on our clothes and equipment was diabolical; bed rolls were in shreds, packs holed and my new boots were now well and truly worn in on the hard granite. I mourned the loss of my trusty Bowie knife somewhere in the kiekie above me; maybe in years to come someone crashing around up there will find it.

The tide was receding as we trudged around headlands which had been impassable only hours before. The long 10 km section from Wekakura Point to Heaphy Bluff is a palm-strewn golden sand beach, divided into three sections by Kotaipapa and Whakapoai Points. The granite here is more of a grey colour that changes abruptly to limestone at the sheer 200-metre Heaphy Bluff—another obstacle that must be scaled.

Instead of returning to the coast, we chose this point to cross over into the Heaphy River valley, and thence to connect with the Heaphy Track. The flood-swollen river defied several attempts to cross, but we eventually found a waist-deep ford several kilometres upstream. Scrambling through some bush, we found ourselves standing on the Heaphy Track, and congratulated each other on our triumph.

We had succeeded, beating the odds. But as well as that, we had achieved the comradeship that only a hostile environment can forge. We had each excelled in different skills, at times rescued and assisted each other, explored and pushed the limits, and witnessed first-hand a terrain few have traversed.

Julius von Haast summed up his journey thus: "I may be permitted to warn persons who are liable to giddiness not to travel by this route, but rather to select that which leads up the Aorere River, and from thence to the Heaphy; but for a man with a stout heart and a strong head, nothing can be more interesting than the journey along this coast, particularly if accompanied by a friend of the same qualities. They may, it is true, meet with disagreeable mishaps, but they will be amply compensated for their troubles by the wild beauty of the scenery, which is such as cannot be described in words."

Indeed.

The last section of the coastal journey, ending up at Heaphy Bluff, was a ten-kilometre stretch of golden sand backed by lush palms. It made for easy walking, but the author (left) and Brian Cooper had to watch out for the occasional extra-large wave.

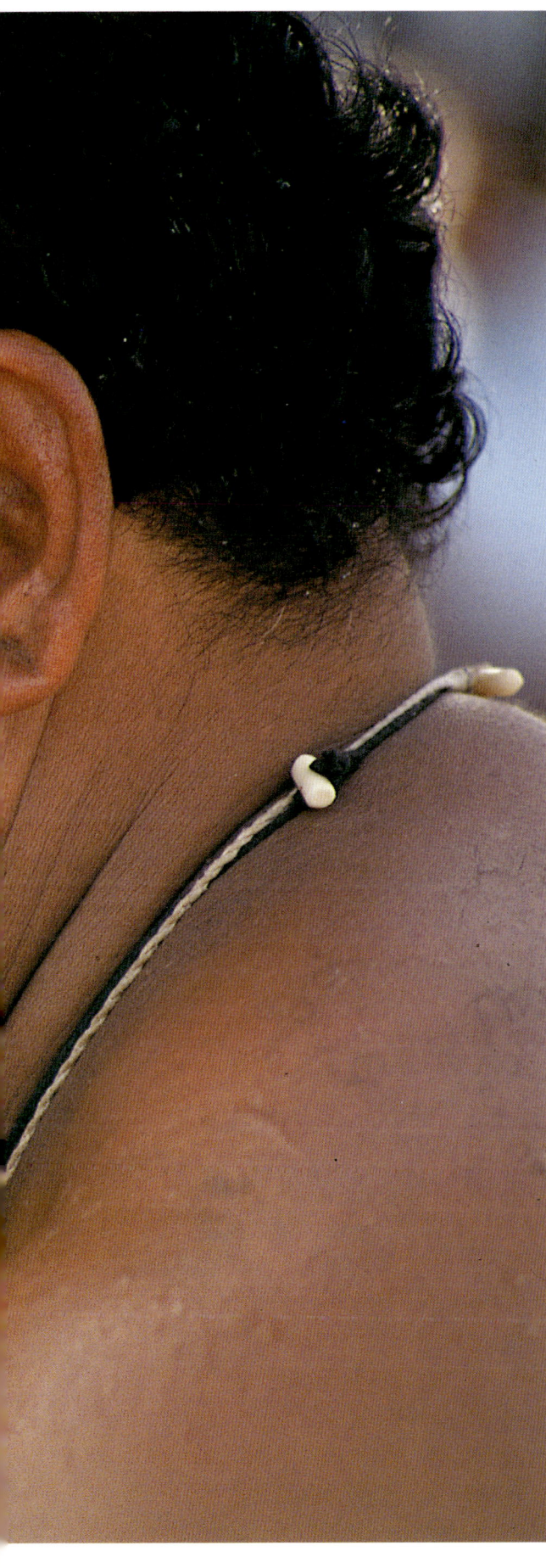

Sharing the breath of life

ARNO GASTEIGER

In Maori culture, the hongi—a pressing of noses—is a sacred act of respect for another person. It represents a sharing of the breath of life, and is a reminder that even something as common as a greeting has spiritual meaning.

The Maori have a saying that runs "Ko te mea nui? He tangata, he tangata, he tangata." What is the most important thing? It is people, people, people.

From the beginning, *New Zealand Geographic* has been about people as much as it has been about penguins or pohutukawa trees. Our writers and photographers have documented the lives of all sorts of New Zealanders—from lighthouse keepers to hot-air balloonists, triathletes to doll-makers, rodeo riders to Polynesian dancers.

In a roundabout way, these articles and many like them have tried to probe the national psyche; to provide insight into the New Zealand character. This focus has been intentional. The magazine was launched at a time when many New Zealanders were thinking seriously about national identity. Did we have one? If so, was it more than the caricature of a country obsessed with rugby, racing and beer?

When the first issue of the magazine went on sale, the 150th anniversary of the signing of the Treaty of Waitangi, the country's founding document, was just 12 months away.

In the lead-up to the 1990 commemoration, Maori embarked on such identity-affirming projects as the construction of a fleet of traditional canoes (see story commencing page 106). This project built on a renaissance in Maori language and culture which had gained momentum over the previous two decades. Large numbers of Maori began to rediscover their roots: their whakapapa (family tree) and their turangawaewae (identity). An awakening to tapu (the spiritual side of life) was leading many to find a renewed sense of mana (prestige).

White (Pakeha) New Zealanders, on the other hand, seemed to be struggling in the lead-up to 1990 to define their own cultural distinctives. What unique flavours could they bring to the celebratory banquet?

Like the Maori before them, European settlers had imported much of their homeland with them: place names, customs, foods, religions, even the plants and animals they had grown accustomed to. They didn't think so much of adapting themselves to an existing culture as implanting their own into virgin territory—this despite the fact that Maori had

DEAN NIXON

Sitting down to a family roast is a time-honoured tradition for New Zealanders. The ingredients of the meal are standard: lamb or mutton, roast potatoes and kumara, peas and carrots, gravy and mint sauce.

been resident in Aotearoa for a thousand years.

As the first waves of settlement rolled on to New Zealand shores in the late 1830s, there seemed every possibility of a productive union between immigrant and native—at least in the early years. However, mutual support and respect were soon eclipsed by a darker colonial agenda of land alienation and Pakeha dominance, leaving a legacy of grievance that is only now being seriously addressed.

Much can be learned about the character of a people from the nature of its pioneers. America was settled by visionaries and idealists, and has retained a measure of those characteristics as national traits. New Zealand colonists were drawn from more stolid working class stock: farmers and tradesmen who detested the English class system and were looking for a chance to be their own bosses.

They certainly weren't afraid of work. They laboured six days in bush, paddock or mine, sawing, ploughing, rooting up the land to unearth gold or gum, and on the seventh repaired their gear—and themselves—before the next bout of work. Among the essential attributes in their isolated settlements were an ability to invent and fix things using limited materials (traditionally a piece of Number 8 fencing wire), to cope, no matter what the hardship, and to be willing to pitch in and help others where necessary.

All these traits have entered more or less into the gene pool of national identity. We are known as a nation of do-it-yourselfers—people who will "have a go" at anything, "give it our best shot" and not be daunted by difficulties. We like to think of ourselves as resourceful, determined, unfazed by opposition. A breezy optimism translates as the "she'll be right attitude" we share with our neighbours the Australians. The confidently spoken "Not a problem!" has become an almost universal reply.

Cocking a snook at the rest of the world and "going it alone" is also an attitude we're proud of. The whole world knows about the country that said no to nuclear ships and no to sport with segregated South Africa. Fewer know that we were also the first to say yes to women's suffrage, and that in the early part of the 20th century New Zealand was regarded as a workers' paradise and the social laboratory of the world.

No doubt the global homogenisation that is the hallmark of the modern age has blurred some of these characteristics. But we can still celebrate the fact that they are part of the mix that makes us New Zealanders—as validly Kiwi as Anzac biscuits and hokey pokey ice-cream, aerial topdressing and the Hamilton jet.

What is needed now is a twining of the Maori and Pakeha strands of identity into a single rope. Or a net, perhaps—a strong multifilament net which incorporates newer lines from Polynesia and Asia as well. A net to harvest the 21st century.

ARNO GASTEIGER

The "great outdoors" have always been a drawcard for New Zealanders, and so too for an increasing number of overseas visitors. River rafting is the sort of wet, wild adventure that today's enthusiastic tourist is likely to opt for.

ARNO GASTEIGER

St John's Ambulance volunteers commemorating Anzac Day—in memory of Allied forces who fought in the two world wars—share a joke during the April 25 parade in Takaka, Golden Bay. Red poppies are worn to mark the day.

PETER QUINN

Hot showers sluice away grime and relax tired muscles at the end of a shift in a West Coast coal mine. Mining has been a way of life in areas such as Reefton and Greymouth for over a century.

following pages: PETER QUINN

On the South Island's West Coast, catching whitebait is more than a hobby or a sport: it's a religion. Whitebaiters at the mouth of the Waita River near Haast use scoop nets to snatch the tiny translucent fish from the surf.

ARNO GASTEIGER

When your world is a 370-foot navy frigate and you share it with 250 others, you take your exercise where and when you can. A scrap of space aft of the flight deck is the ship's gymnasium, where Leading Seaman Jim Wilson works out.

FRANCOIS MARITZ

A wheelchair is no barrier to sporting prowess for Brian Frogatt, who holds the record in the amputees' section of the New York marathon, has represented his country at the Para Olympics and is a triathlete. Archery is just a hobby.

PAUL FISHER

Isabel Harper has been making and selling kewpie dolls and windmills at A&P shows—fun-filled fiestas organised by the country's Agricultural and Pastoral associations—for close to 40 years. The shows are some of the few occasions which bring town and country together.

ARNO GASTEIGER

*The pickings are slim for William Malcolm and wife Lynne, busking on Auckland's main street. The Malcolms know
Queen Street well: their bread-and-butter income comes from recycling cans and bottles picked up off the street.*

ARNO GASTEIGER

The day we "brought it on home." America's Cup fever grips New Zealand, and half a million people line Queen Street to cheer our newest sporting heroes.

following pages:

RALPH TALMONT

Meeters and greeters of many races crowd the entrance hall of Auckland International Airport, the country's main gateway. Tourism is expected to reach three million visitors per year by the turn of the century.

At the bach

By NIGEL COX

Abridged from New Zealand Geographic, *January - March, 1995*

I ALWAYS SAVOUR THE MOMENT when, after a long spell in the city, I finally make it out to my bach. Struggling forward into a head wind as I explore along the high water mark, mopping at a bit of a runny nose, I can't help thinking, "I love coming to this bach"—but why? What is it New Zealanders love so much about their baches?

According to the Big Oxford, bach has its origins in the word *bachelor.* "He's baching," we say when a man lives on his own for a spell, and what we mean is that we expect there won't be a table cloth on the table, or anything much in the fridge, or fresh flowers in the vases. Certainly, in the early part of this century baches were houses where, even if women were present, male domestic standards were dominant. So you had rudimentary apparatus for cooking on—such as primuses—and odd furniture, and tide tables pinned to bare walls; in extreme cases, beer crates to sit on, sacks for curtains, the chimney backed by corrugated iron, a dirt floor.

Manicured beach subdivisions aside, we still seem to like our baches cheap, because we use them only occasionally. Perhaps it's a particularly New Zealand thing to think that a beach house should be rough and ready. Our post-Depression past doesn't have such a grip on us these days, but when the older baches were built most of them belonged to families who didn't necessarily have a great deal to come and go on. A bach, especially one by the sea, offered the promise of food for free along with the pleasure to be had from catching it. And there were no summer fashions to be keeping up with, and few expensive diversions to spend your money on. Here the ethos could be utilitarian, daggy even, and none would object.

The classic bach is by the sea, with an outside toilet and tubs and a galvanized iron tank to collect rainwater off the roof. At the tank-stand a cake of soap and a towel wait beside a white enamel basin. Inside, the walls are unlined, the rafters are exposed and the wiring can be seen snaking around the walls to the power point, which inevitably has four double plugs rising humpbacked from it. The floors are bare boards, stained dark by the sweat of bare feet. On the walls there's a Lands & Survey map, a painting by a hand yet

PHIL CRAWFORD

Hand-me-down appliances, piles of mismatched crockery, an old valve radio: this bach at Whitianga is a classic of its kind.

to produce its masterpiece, a list of dos and don'ts. Instructions abound, as do keys on nails, and stacks of paua shells, and little piles of playing cards, usually two shy of a pack. On a high shelf books of astonishingly diverse character lie as though their search for a final resting place is over.

"Go outside and see how much water we've got left," Dad says. When you tap the side of the tank with the broom handle there's a hollow clank.

You sit on the wooden oval above the long-drop and wonder if a spider will bite your backside.

You read a few pages of an old hardback novel with no dust jacket. *S. Jenkins '54* is inscribed on the flyleaf. No-one in the family has ever heard of S. Jenkins.

A morepork calls in the night, and you step outside. In the complete darkness you stare at more stars than you remembered being up there, and are reminded, now that you're used to it, just how much light they give.

LEONIE JOHNSEN

About as far from the madding crowd as you can get, this secluded retreat at Snake Point in the Marlborough Sounds has been in the photographer's family for 65 years.

in these two baches to talk, argue, read Christmas books on bunks, go for nature walks, introduce spouses, eat paua, moki, greenbone and crayfish, play marathon games of tenniquoits, catch up on gossip, set the nation to rights, fall out with each other, fall back in, lie outside in the darkness and watch for the orbiting satellites which could be seen moving against the fixed points of the background stars.

We're a nation of highly mobile people, so what is the attraction of taking our holidays in the same place year after year? We probably say we go to our baches because there are things we like to do when we're there. But isn't the main attraction that there isn't much to do? Oh, we'll potter with this and that, spend hours lying on the sandspit with the rod tip sawing above us, with the line arcing out into the depths—but are we really trying hard to catch anything?

The most wonderful sensation at a bach is the way that time turns into vast landscapes which move past with the stately calm of continental drift. An hour spent over a single page of the newspaper and a steaming cup, the eyes drifting up from the print to survey the long line of the horizon, where nothing moves. Are those clouds stratocumulus? And so half an afternoon is spent riffling through such reference books (Arthur Mee's encyclopaedia, an ancient *Pears*, a dictionary minus its binding, mostly used for *Scrabble*) as have ended up on the sagging shelf. This desire to satisfy random attacks of apparently trivial curiosity suddenly seems urgent and profound.

And I suspect that perhaps it is. In our baches we have the opportunity to prove to ourselves that "the adaptable man" (or woman) isn't far beneath our skins. Armed with only our intellect, haven't we always thought, we could solve any problem, couldn't we, if only we had the time? And so at baches we try ourselves out as ornithologists, geologists, local historians, meteorologists, marine biologists.

My guess is, this desire to reaffirm ourselves as potential masters of all disciplines is a strong if buried trait among New Zealanders. We like to think that if need be we could wield an axe, steer by the stars, snare a hare—that we're only out of practice in these arts because we're too busy exercising our specialist skills to have time for these more universal ones.

One of the ideas that come up again and again in conversations held in baches is how sane this kind of life is, and why aren't we living out here full-time? In 1949, A. R. D. Fairburn ran a long poem past this notion. *To a Friend in the Wilderness* begins with a catalogue of woes:

> *For God's sake let it rip, let go the rope,*
> *the weight is dead against you. Toss in your hand,*
> *the cards are stacked. You're jostled off course,*
> *get off your horse. Our land*
> *is conquered, lost: homunculus supreme*
> *sits on the world's back: the weevil is in the sack,*

Every New Zealander has been here, has done these things. We enjoy our baches, but we think of them as common-or-garden; they don't seem special to us. In fact, they're as specific and indigenous as Taumarunui on the main trunk line.

My family lived on a branch of the main trunk, lower down the island, at Masterton in the Wairarapa. In 1964 my aunt and uncle bought a bach at a place called Mataikona, a strip of windswept coast north of the lighthouse at Castlepoint, and a few years later my parents bought the bach next door.

All through my teenage years my extended family gathered

MARCEL TROMP

A bach is a feeling as much as a place; a mood of relaxed abandonment, where a game of darts is as important as going *fishing or washing the dishes. The Perkins family has no trouble catching the feeling at their bach near Wellington.*

ALAN DOVE

A single three- by seven-metre
room with a solitary window
looking out over the waves, Jim
and Dea McNulty's bach (or

"crib" as southerners call them)
at Moeraki is about as close to
the tide as you can get without
being in a boat.

and then proffers a solution:

Listen: when Kelly went he left me his boat,
the sun is on the sea and the fish are biting,
the garden is full, the fruit begins to fall.
For God's sake chuck it, join me and share my crust,
the world well lost. Make life a long week-end.

One of the advantages of owning a bach is the way it provides a bolt-hole. This is where we'll come, we think, to lick our wounds. If the sharemarket collapses, if she leaves me, if they drop the bomb, if I go mad. Here I'll be able to survive. I'll live off the land, take my cues from the natural world, and become sane again.

My bach and the others which belong to our family are typical of thousands of others in isolated spots all around the country—at the end of a gravel road, gathering water from iron roofs, with heat for cooking coming from gas bottles. No electricity, no phones, though power poles can be seen advancing.

My uncle, a doctor, originally brought us here because he wanted a get-away where he couldn't be reached by phone. Now, as pagers and cellphones spread their tentacles, that sense of remoteness is getting harder and harder to achieve. Once you could stare out the front windows of our baches all day without seeing a single car to raise the dust; not any more. In the last year we've had to pay for a fence to keep the cows, which have always wandered down through our properties, off the road. In recent years our rates have gone up dramatically. Though the land is rough and the road unsealed, a subdivision has been started at the end of it: concrete kerbs, street lighting, flush toilets.

This process is happening all over the country. As our cities get more densely populated, the desire to escape them intensifies. The government valuation on baches is rising steadily, especially on those within reasonable driving distance of urban centres. Gaps that have been left in the coastline for years are being reassessed as to their development potential. Well, I suppose you've got no reasonable grounds for grumbling if others want to share the paradise you've found—but that doesn't mean you don't grumble.

The problem is, more people means that the place changes. It's not just the cars you've got to listen to instead of the silence. It's that the odd bach or two doesn't affect an ecosystem the way that a community of them does.

Take fishing, for instance. All through my childhood, a visit to the bach meant eating seafood. Each night we'd put out a small net and next morning always had something for breakfast: moki, butterfish, the odd cray. Always. In the last three years we haven't netted a single edible fish.

Of course, we blame the occupants of those baches built since ours was, or those who don't bother to build; who come crawling across the rocks in their hundreds each weekend at low tide, armed with wetsuit and sack. We sit on our steps, behind the wobbling curtain of our gin and tonics, and mutter sour remarks about interlopers.

In fact, these day-trippers probably have nothing to do with the scarcity of fish. At night, using binoculars, we can see the fishing boats out on the horizon, with the great light of the mothership glowing like a flame which all the little craft circle around as they spread and then close the giant net. During the day the professional fishermen speed back and forth in their powerful boats—our pleasure has become their work. It's a theme repeated wherever you glance. Once one of the kids was sent out with togs and a screwdriver to pick up a few paua for fritters; these days you need to dive deep and get lucky. Once the kids made holiday money by collecting agar, a kind of seaweed which is used for making a neutral jelly on which biological cultures are grown; these days people collect

agar for a living.

It's not that these activities shouldn't take place. In this country we've always encouraged the commercial exploitation of natural resources; it's what New Zealand is built on. But the more desperate economic climate and the slow but steady swelling of the population mean that being at a bach gradually becomes more like being at home. In our baches we cook more complicated meals these days, and drink wine from bottles instead of beer from flagons. Progress, I suppose.

At my bach there's a sheep's skull which has nestled in the

MARCEL TROMP

Bric-a-brac and objets d'art seem to gravitate to baches; witness the collection of odds and ends at this bach on the Wellington coast.

tall grass behind the long drop for the past five years. For a while I had it up, sitting on top of a fence post so that it didn't get forgotten, but a guest found it disturbing and it's back in the grass now.

I glance at the post and remember—*memento mori*. It wasn't that I insisted on having a prompt to morbid introspection, but the skull, whitened and hollow, traversed by the faint dark wrigglings where its pieces joined, like writing, like rivers on a map, had been thrown up by the shiftings of the sand, and it seemed unwise to bury it.

Similarly, bones, collected for the windowsill, and the carapace of a crab, and the middens revealed when the wind shifts banks of sand; the past seems to come to you for inspection. Once a piece of cliff crumbled away and there, in cross-section, was the charcoal bowl of an umu. Death, the cycles that life has turned through in this place, rarely enters so tangibly into my city existence.

And the mating cries of the birds, the arrival of their eggs, the gradual feathering of the fledglings, are also cycles we have time to watch. The cycles of sun and moon, the emergence of the stars, the rise and fall of the tides, the morning and evening breezes. It's not even that we focus on these things, but we take them in, just part of the fresh air we're breathing.

Occasionally, the land itself seems to beckon us. Once, as a teenager, pitching with a nine iron towards a sandbank behind the bach, I hit a shank and had to search for the ball way off to the side, among rushes. It had rained heavily the night before and the sand had been moved around, or perhaps it was just the wind. Whatever, I bent down to find that, pointing at me like a finger from the sand, was a length of pounamu. When I drew it forth it was eight centimetres long, and slim, flat along one edge and gently curved along the other. A hole had been drilled in the top end so that a cord might be attached.

At the National Museum the ethnologist told me that this piece of stone was old, pre-European and, when it was in use, was probably serving as a fish-threader. He pointed out a flaw half way along its green side, and said that most likely, with a piece of this size, only partially carved, it was being used for a while to see if it would break. If it broke it would be made into two smaller ear pendants, but if it proved strong it would become a neck pendant of some significance.

Pretty well every bach has a story of this sort to offer, an encounter or discovery or sighting that simply would not have occurred at home. We don't go on holiday to seek these experiences, we don't consciously try to "get back to nature." We just want some time in a place that isn't as dominated by us as the suburbs we live in.

Paul Thompson, author of the only book on baches, estimates that there are probably 40,000 (including "cribs" and "holiday homes") around the shores and in the bush pockets of New Zealand—so they won't be vanishing just yet. But we have a great deal to lose if they do. Baches represent a mood that is in danger of vanishing from this country. They were an expression of freedom: of the openness of a country with a low population, of our impulse to do for ourselves, our freedom from fear of wild animals or extremes of weather.

A good bach is often half-hidden behind low shrubbery or tall, unmown grass. It fades back, has the world at a distance, as we do when we bach it.

> *Let us be done with concrete and steel,*
> *plastic and formica and all the festoonings*
> *of luxury and comfort, all the false triptrap*
> *gadgetry of glamour . . .*
> *. . . give me back the smell of salt and earth and iron*
> *and the sweet wood smell burned grey by the sun.*
> (from *Shack*, by Murray Edmond)

It's easy to romanticise the appeals of the "natural" life, especially as we move from being a nation of rural dwellers to one that lives in cities. But baches can provide a holiday from the city and at the same time remind us of who we are beneath our city skins. Without a bach I would feel I was missing a vital part of the equipment I use to right myself—to set myself to rights, to write right, to get things right.

I don't think I'm alone in these feelings. Baches help us keep one foot in the dirt, to keep our feet on the ground. They seem to be an important part of this country, to belong here; and to be part of our feeling that we do too.

ALASTAIR JAMIESON

Holiday traditions such as an annual children's fancy dress competition have been enjoyed (or endured) by generations of bach dwellers at Baylys Beach, near Dargaville, where a bach community of 17 cottages was established in 1914.

Waka

By BUDDY MIKAERE

Abridged from New Zealand Geographic, *January - March 1990*

I HAD NEVER BEEN on a waka taua before. This one is called Nga Toki Mata Wha o Rua, a namesake of Kupe's canoe, and I'm told that it needs every one of its 80 paddles to push it along.

The canoe is big—nearly 120 feet long. It's carved from the trunks of three kauri trees and sits squat and fat in the water off the beach below Te Tii marae at Waitangi.

The order is given, *"Kia rite!"* All the paddles dip into the water together. *"Tokihi!"* the crew growls. The paddles come out, they clunk a beat on the hull and then dip again. *"Tokihi!"* In, out, clunk! *"Tokihi!"* The waka slowly builds up speed as the paddlers' muscles flex and ripple.

"Tokihi!" Drops of sea water and sweat mingle and run down their back-bones.

"Tokihi!" The kaea, fugleman, holds up his taiaha and raises the tempo. *"Tokihi!"* Now the canoe begins to lift. *"Tokihi!"* To drive through the swells. *"Tokihi!"* In, out, clunk! *"Tokihi!"*

I suddenly feel scared. From this very place last century, Ngapuhi under Hongi Hika, Tareha, Pomare, Waikato—all the great chiefs of Tai Tokerau—set out on their famous raids to the south. Raids against my own people.

I find it hard to sit still among the sweating crew, imagining the despair that must have gripped the survivors of those raids— brought back to this bay in canoes just like this, on calm, peaceful mornings just like this. Some of them would die for Ngapuhi's utu, revenge. Others would become slaves, an even worse fate. As slaves they would be subject to the command of the smallest Ngapuhi child, fed on scraps thrown down in the dirt and forced to fight with the dogs of the pa for even those. Death always just a crack on the head away. A cloud hides the sun.

It is December 1989, and I'm attending the last planning hui for a project that has captured the hearts of Maori people throughout New Zealand: Kaupapa Waka, Project Canoe—a project that has been 50 years in the making.

To mark the centennial of the Treaty of Waitangi in 1940, Te Puea Herangi, leader of the Tainui people of Waikato, wanted to

ARNO GASTEIGER

Vivid reminder of ancestral days, the waka taua (war canoe) of Mataatua tribe leaves Whangaroa Harbour on its journey to Waitangi.

restore and build waka taua. She wanted to express the tribal prestige and unity of all Maori people by building a fleet of seven canoes, one to represent each of the major tribal groups of the country. But World War II intervened, and only three new waka taua were completed, among them the one that I find myself riding in across Peowhairangi Bay: Nga Toki.

"*Tokihi!*" The waka sweeps on. Some of the crew are tiring. But here's a chance for a break. The local tourist catamaran looms alongside. The haka rings out as the crew drive the waka on: "*Au! Au! Aue ha!*" The white blades of the paddles crash against the hull once and then lift into the air together in salute. Nga Toki glides on, suddenly silent, and the tourist cameras click and whirr in a frenzy.

Nineteen-ninety. It's the anniversary of our country's beginnings, 150 years since the signing of the Treaty at Waitangi. Te Puea's waka taua dream has been revived, but on a much grander scale than Te Puea envisaged. This time more than 20 waka taua are to be built or refurbished; some to take part in the opening ceremonies of the Commonwealth Games and other events, but all to meet at Waitangi on February 6.

The organisers say that the Kaupapa Waka project meets two needs. The first is to demonstrate mana Maori, pride in Maori arts, skills, and organisation, and to motivate Maori.

The second is to provide a vehicle by which the majority of ordinary Maori people can contribute to the life of the nation.

"*Tokihi!*" Nga Toki glides in to the wharf at Russell. The crew dig in and lean back hard on their paddles. The water surges around us—Nga Toki takes a power of stopping.

"Y'all come far?"

It's an American woman in a green T-shirt. "Yeah," comes the casual reply. "We left Hawaii last night."

"Oh really! George, did you hear that? Now, I want a picture of these guys."

The green T-shirt pushes George forward, and the crew of Nga Toki loll back in their seats and smile for George's camera.

Kaupapa Waka caused an explosion of activity around the country as various iwi groups began building their waka, training crews and fundraising. It wasn't just canoes that Kaupapa Waka built, but a people. Canoe building is just one of the many aspects of traditional Maori life which have changed dramatically in the last 150 years: the hard labour of hewing trees down and shaping them into canoes using only stone tools and fire is gone forever. Ancient tools have been replaced by chainsaws, steel adzes and chisels, fibreglass, laminated planks, marine paints—the whole gamut of technology.

Master carver Tuti Tukaokao has built three canoes. Te Awanui (47 feet long and 30 paddlers), to be crewed by Ngaiterangi at Waitangi, is his work, as is the design of the whakairo, carving, on Takitimu, the 80-foot Ngati Ranginui waka with room for a crew of 60. Tuti reflects: "With the use of modern tools, a lot of the hard work is taken away. It means

that we can complete jobs quicker. Why should we spend months and months doing work, when with modern tools we can accomplish a lot more?"

Tuti suffers from osteoarthritis. His right arm, the one which swings his mallet, has already been operated on to try and arrest the disease. Modern equipment enables him to practise his craft still.

Te Kotuiti Tuarua, 58 feet long and big enough to carry a crew of 60, is a canoe which belongs to the "modern" tradition that tohunga like Tuti Tukaokao have pioneered. Constructed of laminated kahikatea and totara, Kotuiti is also the first waka taua to be built by the Hauraki tribe of Ngati Paoa this century. For them, Kotuiti is more than just a canoe: it represents a step in the restoration of the mana of their tribe.

That restoration began in 1986, when the government returned to the tribe a 2000-acre farm block on Waiheke Island. This event recognised Ngati Paoa's mana whenua. The canoe was to foster mana tangata. According to Gary Thompson, one of the organisers, "It was brilliant. The young people really committed themselves to it, especially at the building stage where they'd stay on and work late to get the job done. They trained hard, too. Beginning in June 1989, we put 130 through our training weekends—things like working-out with weights, 'dry water' paddling, learning about the different parts of a waka, learning haka and waiata, learning about tribal traditions and about wairua, the spiritual side. When the waka was finished, our kaiako, Jake Puke, made all of us hongi the figurehead on the tauihu. It was a very moving experience, and after that we really felt at one with our waka."

Ngati Paoa decided to take Kotuiti part of the way to Waitangi by sea. The January departure morning was dull, the sky low. As if to compensate, the crew made the ground of their marae at Kaiaua shake with their haka. Down on the beach they circled the canoe, each running a hand around the carved rauawa (sides) in a show of aroha for it.

Kotuiti left the stony Kaiaua beach accompanied by karakia (prayers) and blasts on a puwhaureroa, a traditional shell war trumpet. Then the canoe circled back, the crew raising their paddles in salute as they passed the urupa and Ngati Paoa's ancestral dead. As the karanga of the women floated across the water, the waka turned and set off for Auckland, 52 kilometres away.

Through the morning, Kotuiti made good progress along the coastline, pausing frequently to salute tribal kainga sites and urupa, old and new. Rounding the "corner" into the long passage between Waiheke Island and the mainland, Kotuiti ran into a sou'westerly which had been steadily rising, and was now pushing up a bumpy slop.

Spray drenched the waka crew. Where the tide had been running in favour of the canoe, now it was coming at an angle, which meant the paddlers had to work harder to maintain speed.

GLENN JOWITT

*Pride, determination and
ultimate effort show on the faces
of the crew of Te Kotuiti Tuarua,
waka of the Hauraki tribe of*
*Ngati Paoa. Twenty-two waka
formed a floating guard of
honour for the Queen during
1990 Waitangi Day celebrations.*

ARNO GASTEIGER

The 1990 waka project was as much about rekindling tribal mana as it was about revitalising boatbuilding traditions. Figure on the stern post of Muri-whenua's waka Tinana recalls an important ancestor.

They battled on, but with the wind gusting to 40 knots, Kotuiti sheltered at Maraetai, and successfully completed its journey to Auckland next morning. The crew were received tumultuously at Orakei, the marae of Ngati Whatua.

Of all the waka, only Mataatua's northern waka achieved the original idea of many: paddling their waka to Waitangi. Mataatua was paddled from Doubtless Bay to Waitangi, a distance of more than 100 kilometres.

One proposal, to paddle the 120-foot South Island waka Te Awatea Hou across Cook Strait, was abandoned (although it later made a double crossing). The canoe of the Taranaki people never made it to Waitangi even by road: a burning brake lining on its transporter caused a fire which destroyed the waka completely. Construction delays and bad weather forced the abandonment of plans to paddle other waka to Waitangi.

In a way, the bad weather showed just how much Maori people have moved away from their past. Several people observed that, on a subconscious level, the crews thought of the waka taua as cars—you just hopped in and away you went. But living in the natural world requires acknowledgment of nature's powers of wind and tide, and when the storm god, Tawhirimatea, stalked the skies, the spirit and muscles of even the best crews could not match him.

The Tainui convoy left Ngaruawahia in the early evening of January 31. It consisted of six waka on their transporters, a fleet of over 20 buses, a containerised kitchen and storeroom, and more than 500 supporters and crew in vans and cars. The convoy, traffic officers front and rear, crawled along all night, reaching Waitangi at dawn the following day.

Home for Tainui for the next week was "Tent City," on the flat land above the beach at Waitangi by Te Tii marae. The city's skyscrapers were two huge marquees, one housing Tainui and associated tribes, the other the communal dining room. Smaller tents were marshalled in rows down the back road—most of them supplied by the Army, who were also responsible for handling the catering arrangements.

An army kitchen smells the same wherever you may be, but walk a few yards towards the bridge over the Waitangi River and you're in fairground land, with mobile stalls offering everything from candyfloss to a hangi.

As Waitangi Day came closer, the anticipation and euphoria among crews and supporters became catching. The hopes that Te Puea had had in 1940 were turning into reality in 1990, for almost everyone wanted to talk about the unity among the tribes.

Tribes like Ngapuhi, Ngati Awa and Ngaiterangi, whose tipuna had come to Aotearoa on the Mataatua canoe, had renewed their common ancestral links by cooperating in the building of their respective waka. Ngati Ranginui of Tauranga reaffirmed their close ties with Kahungunu, but more especially with the Tainui tribes, in remembrance of the time when they had fought as allies against the Pakeha during the 1860s.

The massed haka of the Tainui crews made the dust fly. The crew yelled and stamped, and what you felt was the passion of Rewi Maniapoto's words at Orakei: "Ka whawhai tonu matou, ake, ake, ake!" (We will fight on forever!)

Unity had a humorous face, too. When Mataatua had a mishap that pitched several of the 50 crew into the water, it became obvious that the Tuhoe "bush boys" had never learned to swim! They were teased about it for days.

The unity on display was not just at a tribal level. In many waka, heavily tattooed Black Power and Mongrel Mob members paddled together, their rivalry sacrificed for a cause they both believed in. Other waka proudly included Pakeha crew, in recognition of the contribution that many Pakeha had made to the various waka taua projects.

But while unity provided the spiritual strength which created the sweet atmosphere of Waitangi, it was the waka and their crews who were centre stage. Their first big day came on Friday, February 2, when the entire waka fleet paddled together across Peowhairangi Bay to the beach at Waitangi and a massed powhiri.

The giant canoes, their crews making the spray leap with their paddles, raced towards the people thronging the beach. The crowd rushed backwards and forwards, trying to make sure they would be at the spot where their waka would land. People laughed and cried. Old men sat alone with their memories, and several old kuia wept openly as the canoes came.

The waka charged in, answering the karanga of the women, and as the hulls grounded the young men leapt ashore to perform their haka. Just for a moment it was possible to shut out the background of cars, tents, motorboats and all the paraphernalia of modern life, and imagine this beach as it might have been 150 years ago . . . a fleet of war canoes drawn up on the sand, and the ranks of shouting warriors.

The crowds inspecting the canoes hardly thinned as night came and the beach took on a carnival air. Most of the waka

ARNO GASTEIGER

Mataatua's waka was built in two pieces from kauri—a favourite timber for tribes of the north—under the instruction of master carver Hec Busby.

were roped off and guarded by crew members, some of whom explained to visitors the manufacture of their craft and the detail of the carvings.

Ngati Maniapoto's flagship, Maniapoto Mokau ki Runga, looked able to fight off an attack all on its own. The tauihu of this canoe owed as much to fantasy as to tradition. When Maniapoto put to sea it looked as if it had sailed out of a Polynesian *Dungeons and Dragons* saga. On the beach, guarded by paddle-wielding crew, it stopped the crowd in their tracks. It was a scandal, it was appalling, yet such was the power of this great sea monster that people admired it anyway.

At the far end of the line of waka was Takitimu, the Ngati Ranginui canoe from Tauranga. The men in charge of the project, George Rikirangi and Morris Wharekawa, were proud of their "plastic fantastic."

"We had a deadline and the only way we could meet it was to look at a new way of building our waka. We were saved by KZ7. Takitimu is built from the same material—but what a cost! Even though the 1990 Commission gave us a grant of $50,000, we had to find more than three times that amount again ourselves. Some of our people took out personal loans to help with the funding."

Takitimu had a unique "extra" on board. During construction, a Tauranga diver mentioned that he knew where there was an original anchor stone in about 40 metres of water. The stone was retrieved and presented to Takitimu. Too precious to use, it was placed in a carved box filled with sea water to keep its coating of marine growth alive. Sitting in a place of honour amidships, the anchor stone became a mauri, a visible repository of the spirit of the waka.

There was a different, but very moving, spirit about the Moriori waka, Te Rangimata. Made under the direction of tohunga Tim Te Maiharoa from bundles of raupo lashed together, the Moriori waka wallowed at anchor, the sea washing through it. It was plain but functional, and superbly adapted for sailing rough Chatham seas. Te Rangimata made a silent statement about non-aggression, and it was good to remember that assertive pride and competitive identity are not the only mana. The waka looked hopelessly hard to navigate, but, as Maui Solomon, co-ordinator for the Moriori waka project, said, "It'll probably be the safest on the water."

The waka's role on Waitangi Day was to provide a floating guard of honour and escort to the Queen's barge. The crews trained relentlessly, and with impressive discipline. They were subject to a rahui which forbade alcohol. One crew captain explained, "Nothing comes easy, man. If you want to be in our waka you have to learn to do it hard, you gotta concentrate, you gotta live for the waka. You can't do that with a guts full of beer."

Paddling out among the Navy frigates anchored in the bay, crews exchanged formalities with Her Majesty's ships.

ARNO GASTEIGER

Tamatea Arikı Nui, the mighty waka of Hawke's Bay tribe Ngati Kahungunu, lies at anchor off the beach at Waitangi. Exhilarated crew, having participated in a traditional welcome, swim back to shore.

The white-uniformed sailors snapped out their salutes while the paddlers raised their paddles, looking like small forests of white-topped conifers. One canoe captain was piped aboard and made his naval offsider a presentation of his paddle.

Ngati Ranginui in Takitimu made a trip across the bay to Russell. They saluted the town, and then presented a paddle to the dignitaries. Local shopkeepers and residents were so impressed that they brushed aside the crew's intention to buy $100 worth of fish and chips. Lunch was on the town.

Three days out from the big day, disaster struck. Tamatea Ariki Nui, the huge Kahungunu canoe which was over 110 feet long and capable of carrying 150 crew, was in trouble. The waka had been built from two totara sections with a central join, and when it had been drawn up on the beach during the powhiri, the pressure on the join had been too much. The waka had started to break in half. Tamatea was moved to the back beach and screened from public view by tarpaulins to

NATHAN BILOW

The identity of a waka taua is embodied in the carvings on its sides, stern and prow. Paddlers attune themselves to the spiritual aspect of their task by running their hands along the carvings.

preserve its dignity. Night and day, men worked, bolting and welding steel bars over the join to strengthen it. A fibreglass coating completed the job and, on the afternoon before Waitangi Day, Tamatea came floating out into the bay again, to a tremendous haka of celebration from all the waka crews.

Waitangi was tomorrow. But maybe it was the night—in the hour before dawn, when finally the beach was clear—that really belonged to the waka. Some, such as Nga Toki and Te Awatea Hou, were anchored off the beach, facing out to sea in the old way, ready for any enemy. Most were nestled side by

side on the beach, symbolising the peace and unity of the kaupapa. But all of them, lying silently in the night, expressed the spirit of the history and identity of this country, for which New Zealanders have yet to learn the true and natural words: "We are here! We are Maori! We can carry you all!"

Te Tii marae, too, grew in stature at night. A dusty concourse by day, in the dark it reasserted its guardianship of the bay. The great carved pou which mark the place where the northern chiefs met to discuss the Treaty among themselves, stared out over Tent City. They'll remain after the crowd; their spirit was here, and made its choices, in 1840.

Waitangi Day came bright and hot. The islands in the bay were floating on the water. A rising swell pushing in from the open sea looked threatening for those waka with little freeboard, but it seemed these waters would be controlled by sheer determination. One by one the waka slipped away through the waves to take up their stations in the flotilla.

It was a gloriously mixed bunch. Heroes of recent years, KZ1 and KZ7, were there, decked out with flags and bunting. So, too, were champion rowing and surfboat crews, a single sculler and a variety of Pacific Island outrigger craft. A dragon boat in vivid technicolour had difficulty going slow enough to keep position. Further out was a collection of tall ships, their spars providing convenient, if unsteady, lookout posts for crew members, and a swarm of small sailcraft and motorboats jostled for position in the sunlight. Two surfers casually worked over a right-hand reef break at the entrance to Hobson's Beach.

Up at the Treaty House, the signing of the Treaty of Waitangi was being re-enacted before invited VIPs. They sat in suits and picture hats in the covered stand, straining to hear because the sound system faced the ordinary people and the concealed protesters in the open stands. Perhaps that was only right, because it's the people of Aotearoa who need to understand the Treaty more than anyone else if it's to become a force for unity rather than division.

Down by the beach, where the people were in shorts and jandals, there was a different spirit—one that echoed the differences 150 years ago between the traders' settlement of Kororareka and the missionaries' station at Paihia. Up at the Treaty House they had come to see the Queen. Down on the beach they came to see Aotearoa putting on a show for her, symbolised by the 22 waka and their 2000 crew.

And then, suddenly, the Queen's barge was in sight, accompanied by Zodiac security boats and a naval launch. The time of the waka taua had come. Nga Toki and its Tai Tokerau crew turned to escort the Queen into the beach. On she came, past the patiently waiting waka, past the captains standing tall, past all the young men who until now had not known pride, all the young men who had suddenly found themselves. And the descendants of the chiefs who had once been lords of the land lifted their paddles as one in salute.

STEPHEN ROKE

There is even a place for children on a large waka—as bailers. Here, at an annual regatta on the Waikato River, a young crew member wades out to his vessel.

A unique and fragile fauna

ROD MORRIS

National symbol the kiwi is nowhere abundant these days, and this white colour variant is even rarer. There are fears that the kiwi will not survive on the mainland, and will eventually be confined to offshore island refuges.

When author and naturalist Gerald Durrell met his first kakapo (New Zealand's flightless nocturnal parrot) he was so taken with the bird that he wrote, "If naturalists go to heaven . . . I hope that I will be furnished with a troop of kakapo to amuse me in the evening instead of television."

Reactions of amazement and incredulity to New Zealand's wildlife have been recorded by naturalists for as long as they have been stepping ashore on this island ark. So many of our native species seem candidates for Ripley's "Believe It or Not." As well as having the world's only nocturnal parrot, New Zealand has the only alpine parrot, a reptile species that hob-nobbed with dinosaurs, and frogs which cannot croak and lack swimming tadpoles—they develop to the adult stage inside the egg.

We have the world's tallest moss and an insect with tusks like an elephant. We have earth-worms a metre long and carnivorous land snails with shells wider than a cricket ball. Until they became extinct, we had the world's biggest eagle and the tallest penguin.

So "primitive" are some of these species that scientists categorise them as living fossils, prompting one writer to describe the country as "the ultimate storehouse for discontinued zoological models."

The story of New Zealand's flora and fauna is a story of splendour in isolation. Seventy million years ago, the fragment of land which became New Zealand broke away from the supercontinent of Gondwana, and has been adrift ever since. It never received the influx of land mammals experienced elsewhere. Instead, it became a land of birds, reptiles, insects and molluscs—and strange ones at that.

There was the legendary moa, striding through the forests like a giant emu, and an eagle with talons the size of a tiger's claws which preyed upon it. Both have gone, but the moa's relative, the kiwi, lives on, and has become our national symbol and an icon of a unique and fragile fauna. There was also the huia, the only bird in the world in which males and females had differently shaped bills. Sadly, it became extinct within the last hundred years. A fashion

DARRYL TORCKLER

Gotcha! A scarlet wrasse disappears down the gullet of a blue cod in the turbid waters of Fiordland—one of the world's unique diving destinations. Attaining lenghts of half a metre, blue cod form an important southern fishery.

for wearing the huia's black-and-white tail feathers in men's hat bands hastened its demise.

The weta, a spiny-legged cricket as big as a mouse, and, in the case of one species, weighing as much as a thrush, still frequents forests and gardens, rasping its music of the night. It is perhaps the only insect in the world where individual members of a species each have their own unique signature tune.

But for the weta, the tuatara and even the kiwi, the glory days are long gone. These and many other native species cling to a precarious existence in a once-safe land that has been turned into a biological battleground presided over by foreign warlords.

Human carelessness over the last few hundred years has destroyed a balance built up over eons. Introduced mammals are the villain in this story: warm-blooded, fast-breeding, perpetually hungry mammals which have decimated both flora and fauna. Goats, deer, rabbits and possums have forever compromised the forests, while rats, weasels, stoats and even mice have sent species after species to the evolutionary slaughterhouse, or relegated them to island homes for the elderly and ecologically infirm.

Besides introducing mammalian pests, humans have had a more direct hand in the destruction. Large-scale land clearance without the precaution of leaving sufficient untouched forest, wetland and tussock has meant that, even if a species could have survived the depredations of the mammal army, it didn't.

Although what is left may be just the tattered remnants of a unique fauna, a commitment to preserve and restore is now strongly embedded in the national psyche—even if the wherewithal to achieve these goals sometimes lags behind the conservation rhetoric.

New Zealand Geographic aims to present a richly detailed picture of this country's wildlife—from glow-worms to mountain goats, bumblebees to bats—and by engaging people's curiosity about the natural world, to foster respect and spur action.

So far, the spirit of inquiry has led us to probe the secret world of the rock pool and to uncover the graveyards of the moa. To burrow into the forest carpet of lichens and liverworts and to partake of the lip-smacking bounty of edible fungi. Our photographers have spent days floating in mangrove swamps, recording the creatures of the mud as they go about their lives. They have kept watch in caves for bats returning to roost after a night's hunting. They have shivered half-frozen on icy bluffs stalking a herd of tahr, hoping for that elusive chance to capture the mastery of these animal mountaineers on film (see page 126).

Why? Because these creatures are "there"? Certainly that, but also because in studying nature, we can learn about ourselves. We can discover similarities and connections. In the long term, we may find ourselves agreeing with Thoreau that "in wildness is the preservation of the world."

KENNEDY WARNE

The description "one of the world's rarest birds" unfortunately applies to many New Zealand species, including the Chatham Island pigeon, down to fewer than 100 birds. Forest clearance and introduced predators are to blame.

WILL COOPER *(both pictures)*

The land that fringes wetlands like Hikurangi Swamp in Northland has become "forgotten acres"—ignored habitats all too easily appropriated for farming and housing. The common blue butterfly, here waiting for the sun to dry its wings after the pre-dawn dewfall, is one of the species to be found in such places.

RUTH PRENDERGAST

Corroded end of a shipwreck's pipe railing provides cosy room-with-a-view for a crested blenny—a common reef fish in New Zealand waters. Purple jewel anemones add an exotic touch to the furnishings.

MICHAEL SCHNEIDER

This green-eyed "alien" is actually a tiny jumping spider common in home and garden. The large front eyes (there are three more pairs positioned around the head) enable the spider to accurately judge distance when it springs on prey.

GORDON ROBERTS

Sure-footed on crags that would daunt any mountaineer, a young bull tahr checks the whereabouts of his companions on an exposed bluff in the Southern Alps. Himalayan tahr were introduced to the country in 1904.

MICHAEL SCHNEIDER

Short-tailed bat makes an aerobatic descent from its roost tree to the forest floor, where it will forage for food during the night. This and another bat species are New Zealand's only native land mammals.

GEOFF MASON

Moa were among the biggest birds that ever lived, and for millions of years they browsed the forests of prehistoric New Zealand. Now only their bones, deposited in cave sediments, tell the story of this prodigious bird.

MICHAEL SCHNEIDER

Zooming in like a mouse on wings, a bumblebee, "tongue" out in anticipation, prepares to gorge on a favourite food source: tree lucerne. Bumblebees are only now being appreciated for the tireless and effective pollinators they are.

ROD MORRIS *(preceding page)*

Jaws that look as though they have been borrowed from a bolt cutter make short work of a katydid. Although tree weta are not primarily carnivores, they will happily devour insects they stumble across.

DARRYL TORCKLER

*Like necklaces swaying to Pacific
swells, ropes of greenshell mussels
create intriguing alleyways for
cruising fish at Port Charles on
the Coromandel Peninsula.
Mussels are grown in their
millions here and in other
coastal sites in both North and
South Islands.*

Tuatara

By CHARLES DAUGHERTY AND ALISON CREE
Photographs by MICHAEL SCHNEIDER

Abridged from New Zealand Geographic, *April - June, 1990*

HATCHING IS TOO GENTLE a word to describe the birth of a tuatara. Over a period of months, the soft-shelled egg absorbs moisture from the soil, swelling up like a balloon until it is a tight-skinned capsule. Then, using its egg tooth—a sharp-pointed spike on the end of its snout—the baby tuatara punctures the shell, and its wet head literally explodes into view. Over the next few hours a series of abrupt wriggling movements will free the hatchling from the egg that has been its home for the last 12 months.

Few people have observed the hatching of a tuatara, which usually occurs in a cool, dark nest about 15 centimetres below ground. But in 1990, 30 tuatara eggs from North Brothers Island in Cook Strait were hatched in incubators at Wellington's Victoria University, giving scientists the opportunity to observe closely an event that has been happening for more than 200 million years.

Tuatara are the last surviving members of a lineage that stretches back to the Mesozoic—the beginning of the "Age of Reptiles." Their ancestors witnessed not only the immense, terrifying diversity of the dinosaurs, but also geological upheavals that shuffled the continents around the globe like jigsaw pieces. Perhaps they even watched from their burrows as the earth shuddered under the impact of a giant meteorite—a disaster some scientists think occurred about 65 million years ago and led to the extinction of the dinosaurs.

Somehow the "proto-tuatara" survived this cataclysm, hung on during the proliferation of birds and mammals, and eventually gave rise to the modern version, which survives only in New Zealand, and only just. Since humans arrived—about a thousand years ago—tuatara numbers have declined rapidly. They disappeared from the mainland a hundred years ago, and are now found only on a small number of offshore refuges.

The birth in captivity of 30 healthy tuatara may mark a turning point in the long history of the animal, for these juveniles are destined to re-colonise some of the islands from which tuatara have vanished. They are the culmination of a long-term research programme that we hope will turn the tide of fate in the tuatara's favour.

Last representative of a lineage that stretches back 225 million years, the tuatara, a "living fossil," is found only on New Zealand's offshore islands.

Tuatara research is not easy. Access to the islands on which they occur has long been restricted by both weather and New Zealand law. That tuatara are mainly nocturnal and have a lifespan that is longer than the normal scientific career does not make the job any simpler.

Besides rock-climbing skills, and the capacity to survive on dried foods for extended periods, all tuatara researchers require one crucial skill: the ability to catch the subjects of their study.

Tuatara emerge at dusk from their burrows and spend most of the night near the burrow entrance, waiting for a tasty meal such as a large weta or lizard to wander within striking distance. Sometimes they forage away from the burrow, perhaps on sun-warmed rocks near the high tide mark, where lizards are also searching for a meal. Spotlit by the beam of a torch, a tuatara will do one of two things: turn tail and scuttle down the nearest burrow, or freeze like a possum. Fortunately, most

The closest most people get to a tuatara is a glimpse at the zoo or a flash of silver when counting out small change. This juvenile tuatara, about two years old, encounters its graven image.

choose the second option. A quick grab around the neck, just behind the powerful jaws, and the capture is successful.

Some of us have learned the hard way that a moment's carelessness may exact a painful price: a bite from teeth honed over tens of millions of years for grasping prey securely, crushing it in powerful jaws and shearing it apart even as it struggles to escape. When a tuatara clamps its sharp teeth into your bare finger, the searing pain endures until the tuatara finally decides to let go—which may be 15 minutes, because the tuatara has nothing if not patience.

Bites aside, tuatara can be very difficult to hold. Large males, the biggest as long as your arm and weighing over a kilogram, can put up a real fight, clawing and thrashing and grunting fiercely. Equally often, however, the tuatara is almost docile, displaying a stoicism that seems somehow appropriate to its antiquity.

Often, no tuatara at all can be seen during the day—they are wary and rarely venture from their burrows. Then, the only way to get one is to go in after it. Lying face down on the dirt, you slowly reach your arm into the burrow, searching blindly and gingerly for the soft skin of a tuatara— often hoping you find nothing at all!

The word tuatara means "spiny-back" in Maori. The spines, like the skin, are surprisingly soft, much like cool, dusty linen cloth to the touch, and pose no threat. If you are lucky, your hand lands on an exposed tail or leg or, best of all, the spines and back. Then, you press the tuatara firmly to the ground, securing it until you get a grip strong enough to pull the reluctant reptile out of the burrow. If unlucky, you find nothing, or you may just touch a tuatara as it retreats beyond your reach. Or, something may grab you. Petrels and shearwaters often use the same burrows as tuatara, and have strong bites if disturbed. Worse, large centipedes with painful, poisonous bites also share burrows with birds and tuatara.

Bitten or not, a visit to a tuatara island is the experience of a lifetime. Few people ever get the opportunity, though, because tuatara have been fully protected since 1895, and permits to land on their home turf are not given lightly.

But what astonishing places these islands are! Many, like Stephens Island (Takapourewa) in Cook Strait or Tawhiti Rahi and Aorangi Islands in the Poor Knights, rise straight up from the sea like stark, primeval fortresses. Cliffs a hundred metres high are topped with thick carpets of wind-shaped scrub: taupata, ngaio, or mahoe. In spring, the northern islands are red with flowering pohutukawa and, on a few islands, the glorious Poor Knights lily.

Signs of life are everywhere. The soil is usually bare from continual digging and trampling by birds and tuatara, and is riddled with burrows. But the scrub is thick, and we often have to crawl under or through the brittle, scratching branches. The combination of forest, soil and bird droppings gives the area a distinctive, pungent bouquet. Particularly ripe is the smell of a blue penguin nest, full of decaying faeces and the remnants of fish and squid regurgitated by the parents as food for the young.

As night approaches, there is an explosion of life. Most tuatara islands are free from mammals, and thus teem with birds, lizards, weta and beetles. From August to November, when seabirds return for breeding, the night-time cacophony of tens of thousands of these creatures creates a wall of noise. Sleep is almost impossible, not only because of the din, but because petrels crash-land on your tent with monotonous—

ROD MORRIS

After hatching, tuatara rely on their own efforts to feed themselves. Here two cryptically coloured juveniles share a large grub. As tuatara age, they lose the strong fawn and brown dappled markings, and become speckled.

but nevertheless startling—regularity. Then, just as you manage to doze off with the approaching dawn, an army of raucous penguins marches past your tent on its way to the sea.

Tuatara islands differ dramatically from the New Zealand that humans have created with their cities, highways, farms, orchards and exotic forest. The forests are silent because the birds that once teemed in them have been killed by rats, cats and stoats, the trees themselves dying because of possums. To visit a tuatara island is to travel backwards in time for a thousand years, or a million, or ten million, to a time when most of New Zealand shared the extraordinary biological diversity now found only on those few offshore islands where introduced mammals are absent.

On Stephens Island, in Cook Strait, the average tuatara weighs 400-500 grams, and in some places as many as 2000 tuatara share one hectare of the forest—almost a tonne of tuatara per hectare. Even in poorer habitats, numbers are as high as 500 per hectare. Such numbers are possible only because the soil, enriched by the tens of thousands of fairy prions that return to Stephens each year to breed, supports a diverse biological community that tuatara see as an enormous buffet.

Anything that moves is fair game to a tuatara: earthworms, beetles, lizards, frogs, weta, injured or juvenile prions, and even, as our colleague Mary McIntyre discovered, young tuatara. Young tuatara have long been a mystery, because they are seen so infrequently, even on islands where adult numbers are high. To discover where the young hide, Mary taped small spools of cotton thread to the tails of a few juveniles and tied the ends of the threads to nearby plants. As the juvenile moved about, the thread unwound behind it, leaving a complete track of all its movements.

Unexpectedly, she found they were most likely to move about in the daytime, despite the danger of overheating or drying out. The reason soon became apparent: "I followed the thread trail of a year-old tuatara that disappeared under a rock in the lighthouse keeper's sheep pasture. Gently lifting the rock to find the juvenile, I was shocked to see the thread disappearing into the mouth of a large adult male along with the tip of the tail of the young one!" Mary concluded that adult tuatara are probably an important predator of baby tuatara, which may explain why juveniles are most active in the daytime, seeking shelter at night when adults are foraging for food.

Tuatara are extremely slow-growing, reaching reproductive maturity between ages 10-15 and continuing to grow until age 30, and living for at least 60-70 years. No one knows how old tuatara are capable of living, but it is entirely possible that the biggest, oldest tuatara on Stephens Island watched Captain Cook sail by in 1769.

Much of our research on Stephens Island has focused on the breeding behaviour of tuatara. Clearly, the survival of any species depends on successful reproduction, and if we can improve reproductive success, we are in a good position to keep the species off the endangered list.

Females choose open spaces in which to nest, which is why an island such as Stephens, cleared for farming last century, supports such a large tuatara population. Mike Thompson, an Australian turtle expert who was helping us with our research, describes the nesting activity he observed: "The females come from hundreds of metres away, spend several days or even weeks digging a shallow nest hole, and then lay about ten eggs in it. Once the eggs are laid, the female fills the nest hole with soil and grass, returning to it nightly for up to a week. Females even appear to guard the nest, presumably from other females, who have been seen digging up other females' nest holes to use for their own eggs."

To hold a tuatara is to be forced, inevitably, to contemplate history. Not only the history of that individual, but the history of its ancestors in New Zealand and even before, when New Zealand was part of the ancient continent of Gondwana. For tuatara are the great survivors in New Zealand. Their ancestors, the first sphenodontidans (a name meaning "wedge tooth"), shared virtually all continents with dinosaurs. They appear as fossils from North America, Europe, England and Africa, from 225 million years ago until about 120 million years ago. Most are smaller than tuatara, and they would not have threatened the reptilian giants with whom they shared the Earth. About 80 million years ago New Zealand broke free from Gondwana, not long before the last of the dinosaurs disappeared. Mammals then began their spectacular evolutionary rise, dominating all continents except Antarctica ever since.

For reasons unknown, the sample of animals stranded on New Zealand as it drifted northward through the Pacific, away from Antarctica and Australia, differed (or came to differ) from those that survived or prospered on the other southern continents. Most importantly, no terrestrial mammals survived in New Zealand. Nor did land snakes or tortoises. But the ancestors of tuatara did, and in the absence of mammals

Zoologist Charles Daugherty, here examining tuatara on the Brothers Islands, believes that a rehabilitation programme for offshore islands is an urgent priority. In the past 20 years, two tuatara populations have become extinct.

they thrived.

New Zealand is famous for its giant extinct birds, but research in the past decade shows that prehuman New Zealand was as much the land of reptiles as of birds. Most spectacular was the giant gecko, *Hoplodactylus delcourti*, as large as a possum, and possibly the taniwha of Maori legend. The rich lizard faunas of many offshore islands and a few mainland locations show that lizards can be extraordinarily abundant. In some sites today, numbers are as high as 4000 per hectare, even with mammalian predators. They could have been even higher a millennium ago.

So, when the first Polynesians stepped ashore in New Zealand a thousand years ago, they would have confronted a relict fauna from the Age of Reptiles. Their first meal of New Zealand food was as likely to have been tuatara as birds or shellfish. And from then until today, the effects of humans and their mammalian followers—rats, dogs, pigs, goats, cats, stoats—were as disastrous for reptiles as for birds, frogs, weta, and virtually all other ancient New Zealanders.

But the tuatara has survived. Just as the ancestors of tuatara escaped extinction through the good fortune of finding a last refuge in New Zealand, so the tuatara itself has survived by finding refuge on a few coastal islands, some barely the size of a tennis court.

During hundreds of years of Maori occupation of New Zealand, tuatara numbers probably declined steadily, but when Europeans arrived, tuatara were still found on both main islands. (None has ever been known from Stewart Island.) Maori hunting seabirds must have known tuatara all too well—a hand thrust down a bird burrow in search of a meal might frequently have been withdrawn with a tuatara attached instead. And while it may have been an important food item for some tribes, the tuatara, like the lizard, was regarded with respect, as an embodiment of supernatural powers.

No member of Captain Cook's expeditions records having seen tuatara. Early Europeans called them "guana," "the great fringed lizard," and "the tuatara lizard." It was a full 50 years after Captain Cook's first landing before the species came to the attention of science, and then another half century before scientists realised it was not a lizard at all, and its full significance as a "living fossil" began to be appreciated.

Much remains to be learned about tuatara, especially its requirements for survival. On fewer than a dozen islands are tuatara populations reasonably secure. As with many other New Zealand species that survive only on offshore islands, the tuatara's future may be precarious for many decades.

Fortunately, the respect, perhaps awe, which the later Maori accorded tuatara is shared by increasing numbers of modern New Zealanders, whatever their origins. Even more respect, combined with vigilant conservation care, is required to ensure that the tuatara has a chance for a future as long as its past.

Looking as ancient and primeval as its extinct relatives the dinosaurs, a large male tuatara makes an impressive sight in the forest on Stephens Island in Cook Strait. Here there are an estimated 30,000 tuatara—more than on all the other tuatara islands put together.

Kea

By PHILIP TEMPLE
Photographs by MICHAEL SCHNEIDER

Abridged from New Zealand Geographic, *October - December, 1994*

• IN SEPTEMBER 1983, the old Pompolona Hut on the Milford Track was destroyed by flood when the pent-up Clinton River broke through its winter avalanche dam. The walking track season was only six weeks away. Planners, builders and helicopter crews worked night and day to complete a new hut complex before the first walkers arrived.

The local clan of kea took a keen interest in all this frantic activity after a cold and quiet winter. Just what were these people up to? One bird, for whom building materials seemed to hold a particular attraction, began stealing nails. So persistent was the bird's thievery that an exasperated carpenter chased it (in vain) over the roof of the new main hut. While his back was turned, another kea stole his packet of roll-your-owns, shredding tobacco and papers to the raucous approval of spectator kea perched in nearby trees.

Weeks later, after the new hut had been completed, the purloined nails were discovered. They had been neatly laid in the gutters of an outbuilding's iron roof, sorted according to size.

Such stories about kea, the "clowns of the mountains," are an inescapable part of South Island high country lore. It is hard to conjure up an image of our mountains without them—these rough, tough parrots with an eye for the main chance, delighting everyone with their monkey-like antics. But there is a darker side to this screeching joker.

In August 1992, television producer Rod Morris, on location at Glenorchy for a documentary about kea, finally filmed what high country farmers have been telling a sceptical outer world for more than 100 years: this one-kilogram, half-metre-long parrot attacks, and can kill, sheep. From a camp high in the winter snows, Morris and his crew recorded kea harassing a merino wether during the early hours of the morning. The footage shows the birds perched on the sheep's rump, dipping into a gaping wound in the animal's back. They are feeding on live flesh and blood. Caught red-beaked. Now high country farmers can say, "We told you so. Look what the kea have been doing to our flocks. See the damage and suffering they cause. They must be controlled."

Inquisitive and intelligent, the cocky kea, the world's only alpine parrot, finds humans and their cast-offs every bit as intriguing as we find it.

For most of the last 130 years, high country farmers, with the support of sympathetic government agencies, have been "controlling" kea. Conservatively, 150,000 have been killed in the name of protecting sheep. Some retributive killing continues even now, but, since the kea was given full protection in 1986, many farmers have cooperated with the Department of Conservation (DOC) in trying to solve the long-standing "kea problem." It could be that the real problem will be keeping this bird off the endangered and, ultimately, extinct list. It is estimated that fewer than 10,000 are left.

Kea have been part of my life since my first climbing trip into the Southern Alps. In September 1959, as we trudged through heavy spring snow up a tributary of the Waimakariri River, a bird flew overhead, flashing its scarlet underwings.

"Is it a hawk?" I asked my companion, observing the hooked beak and powerful claws.

"No. A parrot, I think," an opinion which seemed confirmed by the bird's unmusical screeching.

"Funny place for a parrot," said I. Even at this dawn of my ornithological knowledge, an alpine parrot seemed an avian oxymoron.

As I spent more time in the mountains, I grew to expect from each trip a lesson from kea about flying or foraging or just getting about in the world above the forest. I watched kea soar on thermals and gully updraughts, their effortless circling making mock of my clumsy alpine stumbles. They woke me with dawn screechings down the chimneys of musterers' huts, and stole my socks when I wasn't looking. They pulled at my pack straps as I rested and tossed stones at me while I lay still and silent in twilight tussocks.

Hanging from the guttering in nor'west rain, they kept an eye on my early creative endeavours as I sat scribbling in an Arthur's Pass bach. I watched them learn to open windows by lifting casement arms, slide back ranchslider doors and remove the heavy wooden lids of rubbish bins by rocking as a team on their edges. I quickly formed the belief that kea were not the clowning fools they appeared at first sight, and had a firm grasp on alpine survival.

At Arthur's Pass in the early 1960s I met the awkward and reclusive chemist Dick Jackson, who seemed, single-handedly, to be finding out what made kea tick. Mountaineers thought he was a bit strange, wandering alone in the mountains, obsessed with birds. Jackson could catch kea by sliding his hand up branches and nabbing them from behind at their blind spot. He banded over 600 of them, enabling him to make the first records of kea range and movement. They proved to be generally homebodies, though sometimes the Jackson birds were sighted or recovered up to 40 kilometres away from the Pass.

Jackson found dozens of kea nests, confirming that they preferred sites at or near the timberline, in natural caves formed by old moraines or in rock and slip debris. It seemed that the high location of kea nests contributed to the bird's ability to survive the depredation of introduced predators such as stoats.

Jackson vigorously advocated that kea were not the meat-hungry harriers and scavengers that sheep farmers made them out to be; that they were only vegetarians who enjoyed the occasional grub or lump of butter.

The kea, *Nestor notabilis*, shares its genus with the kaka, another New Zealand parrot that conforms much more closely in its bill shape, diet and forest behaviour to parrots in Australia and New Guinea. We may never know how many million years ago *Nestor* arrived here, or exactly when a variant subspecies of our original proto-parrot took to the hills to begin the kea line. But this process of alpine adaptation seems consistent with mountain-building processes in the South Island which began between 10 and 15 million years ago.

Kea populated the North Island during the last ice age more than 10,000 years ago, when much of the North Island south of the 38th parallel had an alpine or subalpine environment. Lore collected by Elsdon Best in the 19th century indicated that the kea survived in the North Island high country until after the arrival of the Maori, but it has been seen there only as a straggler in European times.

Kea went into the European record books when Walter Mantell collected a specimen in Southland in the early 1850s. As surveyors, prospectors and farmers moved into the South Island high country in the years following, they reckoned the kea's range was extending further and further north, though it is more likely that they simply hadn't travelled the country enough to see it. By 1904, it had been recorded in all the southern ranges from Nelson to Fiordland.

The attitude of most 19th century Europeans to both the kea and its environment is exemplified by Samuel Butler's account of exploring the headwaters of the Harper tributary of the Rakaia River in 1860. In his classic, *A First Year in Canterbury Settlement*, he wrote, "This bush, though very

Data on the age, sex and behaviour of "troublemaker" birds on South Island skifields should pave the way to a more peaceful coexistence between humans and kea.

Kea have quickly learned that where humans go, a free meal usually follows. They have also learned to get their claws and beaks into just about every conceivable form of mischief. Among their specialities are stripping the rubber from car doors and windscreen wipers and trashing roof racks.

ROD MORRIS

For over a century, a bounty hung over the head of the kea, which, it was claimed, harassed and even killed sheep. Over 150,000 birds were shot, although few were ever sighted "in the act," and many people doubted that the playful bird was capable of such delinquency. This incriminating image—the first to be recorded on film—proved that kea attack sheep.

beautiful to look at, is composed of nothing but the poorest black birch . . . There was a kind of dusky brownish-green parrot, too, which the scientific call a Nestor. What they mean by this name I know not. To the unscientific it is a rather dirty looking bird, with some bright red feathers under its wings. It is very tame, sits still to be petted, and screams like a real parrot. Two attended us on our ascent after leaving the bush. We threw many stones at them, and it was not their fault that they escaped unhurt." Here ended a lesson that kea took only a few generations to permanently absorb. They don't come close enough to be petted now.

On the way back, Butler and his mate "burnt the flats, and made a smoke which was noticed between fifty and sixty miles off." For kea, the burnings which occurred up and down the eastern slopes of the Southern Alps were nothing less than catastrophes. And after the fires came thousands of woolly mammals that scoffed every remaining succulent shrub and berry in sight. For tens of thousands of long-lived, principally vegetarian parrots, the prospects were bleak.

First signs of a new sheep "disease" were reported by shepherds on the Lake Wanaka Station in 1867. But what were first taken to be sores in the loin area of sheep were soon seen to be wounds caused by an unidentified animal. Dogs, hawks and gulls were progressively discounted until the initially ridiculed suggestion that the "Nestor parrot" could be responsible was finally confirmed by eyewitness accounts.

The cause of death of many sheep was early identified as a virulent kind of blood poisoning caused by *Clostridium* bacteria transmitted by the kea's beaks. Scores of sheep would die overnight, often from minor wounds. The reason for the kea attacks was put down to the fact that they had acquired, through their natural curiosity, a taste for sheep meat and fat from carcases hung on station gallows before human consumption, or from skins tossed over fences to dry.

Researchers admitted that kea were probably driven by hunger to investigate and attack sheep, especially during winter when natural food was scarce. The question they failed to ask was, what did all those kea eat during winter before there were sheep?

Recent research reveals that kea, like most birds, need a regular intake of naturally occurring lipids (fats) to provide easily stored energy. Some montane and subalpine plants, such as snow totara, are rich in vegetable lipids, and it is no surprise that these are among the kea's favoured foods. Take away plants like snow totara through burning and grazing, and kea get hungry, whether it is winter or not.

Kea not only faced competition for food from sheep on the high tussock grasslands, but also, from about the turn of the century, increasing competition in the forests and subalpine regions from introduced deer, chamois and goats, which reached plague proportions. Then there was the direct mortal threat of weasels and stoats originally brought in to deal with

acclimatised rabbits, which had further destroyed the tussock grasslands. More recently, there has been devastation of the forests by possums.

Kea faced ecological disaster on a large scale. It is not surprising they fought back as best they could. They needed the nourishment that sheep and other mammals, dead or alive, could provide.

The farmers who had unwittingly exposed their sheep to death and maiming knew just what to do. Kill the killers.

In short order, the kea became New Zealand's Canadian wolf or Tasmanian tiger, Public Enemy Number One, to be exterminated at all costs, shot and poisoned. A bounty was put on kea beaks, financed by run holders, county councils and the Department of Agriculture. The value varied over the years, but in the 1920s it was ten shillings per beak: five shillings from the government and half a crown each from run holder and county. The ten shillings of 1925 is the equiva-

lent today of $65—a clear incentive to full-time hunting.

The bounty stayed on until 1970, when the kea was granted partial protection. An estimated total of 150,000 kea killed in the 100 years from 1868 can be easily sustained.

This is one of the worst cases of avicide in history. That the kea survived this massive slaughter, and the continuing pressures on its environment, seems little short of a miracle. Better, its survival is a tribute to both its physical resilience and a level of intelligence that has enabled it to adapt to a radically altered ecology and to exploit whatever new oppor-

The kea's survival in harsh alpine conditions is largely due to its physical equipment: raking talons, a beak more versatile than a Swiss army knife and an eye for the main chance.

tunities have presented themselves for food gathering, chiefly through human agency.

Even as recently as the mid-1980s, attitudes towards the bird were polarised. Conservationists and animal lovers viewed the continued killing of kea as barbaric and unacceptable in an age which placed increasing value on New Zealand's diminishing and unique indigenous wildlife. High country farmers stuck to their right under partial protection to destroy kea which molested their sheep.

From the 1960s, kea also came into conflict with operators in the burgeoning skiing industry. In anthropomorphic parallel, it seemed that immature males were causing most of the trouble. The youngsters were seen as playful clowns when they rode the wind-driven ventilators on the tops of buses, pushed volleyballs around with their heads or skated down roofs. They quickly became pests when they stripped the rubber from car windscreen wipers and doors or the insulation from power lines, and emptied out rubbish containers. Less tolerant skifield operators shot the offenders.

Visitors to the mountains who enticed kea with food for entertaining photo opportunities stoned them when they stole lens caps or gloves. And the kea killed themselves, choked by ingested plastic, drowned in water tanks and poisoned from chewing lead-head nails. But the skifield huts and rubbish dumps had become another source of easy takeaway food. Life was hard and dangerous in the fast lane.

A turning point came in 1986 when conservationist pressures led to full protection for the kea. In exchange for giving up their legal right to shoot kea, farmers received an undertaking from the Wildlife Service and its successor DOC that its officers would investigate all reports of kea attacks and take action. This would usually amount to accurately identifying problem birds and either removing and relocating or destroying them.

The same deal applied as a last resort to skifield operators, though these would be encouraged to minimise damage to equipment and buildings by making them safe from the kea's powerful, investigative beak. A balance, at last, seemed to have been struck between conservation of the kea and protection of human high country interests.

At the Remarkables Skifield, near Queenstown, I look over the thronged beginner slopes and the international lunch crowd on the cafeteria verandah. As kea hop among the tables, scavenging chunks of pie and lapping up soft drink, manager Andy Chapman says, "I think their place is very definitely here. You can see that in the reactions of our guests to the keas. There is a symbiotic relationship. Here is one of the few opportunities that skiers from Japan, the States, even New Zealand, have to get close to a bird in an alpine environment. It is literally a native clown."

What about damage to equipment? Chapman thinks that in the first years of operation, the kea was not given a great

deal of consideration. Safety circuit cables on ski lifts were damaged, junction boxes on the towers were broken open and the colourful resistors picked out. Since then, "kea proofing" of the skifield has been carried out progressively over a number of years. Vital equipment has been stoutly sheathed or encased, rubbish bins have been secured, even the rope of flag halyards replaced by wire.

As I plug up a steep snow gully through the Remarkables' crags I reflect, with a lightening heart, on Chapman's remarks. They mark a fundamental shift in thinking about kea—an acknowledgement that they have rights in a mountain environment that has been radically altered for the benefit of humans. At least the rights of coexistence.

Ahead of me, Queenstown conservation officer Rudi Hoetjes stops and listens to his headphones as he tracks the slopes with a radio scanner. He has picked up a male kea carrying a tiny transmitter. "Sounds like he's close to the nest site," he says.

The kea's eyrie is superbly situated, at the top of a sheer and sunny north-facing rock wall. We take turns to jam ourselves in a position from where we can peer down the entrance tunnel. A squawk tells us that the hen is home.

By the light of a torch we see movement beneath her breast feathers as she squats on a tussock nest. "She's got chicks!" Rudi grins and waves me away. Time to go before we create a disturbance. High above on a rock pinnacle, the cock keeps an eye on us. Like all good kea cocks, he ensures his mate and offspring have a regular supply of tucker, often from the rich pickings among the skifield lunch tables. Symbiosis indeed.

On the way down, I take my time, admiring the snow-drenched view, and think about kea surviving ice ages, fires and guns. I think about the continuing pressures on their environment and day-to-day existence. I think, despite people like Andy Chapman, who believe kea are as natural in this world as the sky and the rocks, that its survival from human depredation is far from secure. We are still too prone to think that the value of our property—whether sheep or windscreen wiper—comes first. The kea, like so many other creatures, suffers from the arrogance of human materialism.

I look back up the mountain and see the cock kea gliding down to his nest, no doubt to check on his mate and chicks after our visit. I reflect that the kea is a rare bird not for its physical characteristics or for its scarcity—as with the kakapo or takahe—but for its indisputable intelligence, and I find it no great leap in judgement to claim it as the most intelligent bird around. If only for its flair and flamboyance and sheer cussedness in the face of daunting odds—yes, its "Kiwi ingenuity"—it demands admiration and respect.

I decide that kea are neither clowns nor killers, not monkeys or wolves. They are just arch-opportunists, omnivorous and adaptable. Perhaps that is why we both love them and hate them. They reflect the best and worst in us.

Kea nests are usually well hidden at the end of a long entrance tunnel between boulders or inside a decaying log. Between two and four eggs are laid, and the resulting chicks depend on their parents for food for up to five months.

Possum

By STEFAN SEITZER
Photographs by ARNO GASTEIGER

Abridged from New Zealand Geographic, *January - March, 1992*

"VHAT'S ALL SE DEAD ANIMALS on se road?" asked the hitchhiker, settling into the passenger seat of the old Falcon.

"Possums," the driver answered briskly. "Haven't they got these little buggers where you come from?"

"No. Vhat's a possum?" asked the foreigner.

"By crikey," the driver shouted above the roar from a muffler that was more hole than metal, "doesn' even know what a possum is!"

Amused by the ignorance of his passenger, the driver sat chuckling behind the steering wheel. By this time the hitchhiker had noticed a strong smell in the car, but decided not to comment on it because the noise of the vehicle had become deafening, making further conversation impossible.

Suddenly the car swung off the highway to follow a metalled side road. The young traveller from Germany didn't like the idea of leaving the main road, and possibly having to walk for miles to get another lift. And the dust—that was another new experience for him. There weren't many dirt roads in Germany, and certainly not many cars so badly rusted through that they sucked dust like a vacuum cleaner.

The road went on for miles—too many miles for the hitchhiker's taste, and soon suspicion started to creep into the young man's mind. His hand went down to his right boot, where he was keeping a piece of cutlery with which to defend life and backpack.

The car pulled into a driveway, carried on over a rough farm track and coughed to a stop at a huge old woolshed.

The driver reached a burly hand over to his passenger.

"Anyway, Jim's the name," he said.

"Pleased to meet you," replied the foreigner, and they shook hands.

"So you don't know what a possum looks like, eh? Well, come and have a look at this."

Jim slid open the door of the woolshed. "Hang on a tick. I'll just crank up the old kero lamp."

Moments later, a lantern that looked as if it had been stolen from Ali Baba and his gang threw its hissing light on to a remark-

Menace with the face of a teddy bear, the brushtail possum is destroying New Zealand's forests—particularly the spectacular pohutukawa tree.

In today's depressed fur market, it is difficult for trappers such as "Possum" Bill McCabe of Morrinsville to make a worthwhile living. McCabe's best tally is 700 possums in a night.

able scene. The floor was strewn with piles of possum skins, spilling out over full wool presses and lying in bundles of different colours and sizes. Dangling from the ceiling were a couple of hundred wooden frames which had drying skins tacked on to them on both sides. Nearby was an enormous workbench on which lay an assortment of scraping tools and remnants of flesh and fur. Somewhere in the midst of all this was a sink, a pile of dishes and an unmade bed.

It was all quite an eye-opener for a young greenhorn from overseas, and little did I suspect then that Jim and his possums would play an important part in my life.

Back in Germany, I had just finished a degree in music, and my delicate fingers were more used to the fretboard of a classical guitar than to the drying boards of a possum trapper. But as I stayed with Jim and began to learn the ways of the bush, boyhood dreams of living close to nature started to become reality.

The more I saw of possums, the more they fascinated me. Marsupials aren't the smartest of mammals, yet hadn't this little critter sidestepped everything *Homo sapiens* could throw at it? Introduced only three years before the Treaty of Waitangi, this furry overstayer now reigns from Stewart Island to Cape Reinga, and has a population on the Chathams for good measure.

While its mocking laugh drives orchardists crazy, other people are enchanted by its cuddliness. Some drivers aim for them on the road; others pick up the wounded and take them home as pets.

Both attitudes are understandable. I remember the first time I came face to face with a possum that wasn't flattened on the road or tacked out on one of Jim's drying boards. I found it quite hard to accept that these cute animals were the focus of the biggest eradication campaign this country has ever seen. To me, the possum looked like a South Pacific version of the teddy bear.

Its big, dark eyes speak of naive innocence, the little pointed nose hosts a crop of shiny, oversized whiskers, and the fact that the female has a pouch makes the attraction irresistible. Imagine all the little treasures a three-year-old toddler could hide in a furry pouch like that. And if you've ever watched a possum eat, you'll know how captivating they are, holding their food in their "hands" like we do, as they munch away.

Far superior to the teddy, I thought.

But the more you see of what this animal does, the less appealing it begins to look. Each cat-sized possum has a seemingly limitless appetite for plant matter—tasty native New Zealand plant matter—and the damage is everywhere: once-green forests now look grey, magnificent canopy trees sometimes over a thousand years old are reduced to "stags' heads" of dead branches, birds that once filled the bush dawn with song are rarely heard now, their supplies of nectar-filled flowers and juicy berries thieved after dark by the voracious intruders.

Animal lovers or not, most New Zealanders agree that drastic action is needed to get rid of the pest. Ironically, it is only now that the magnitude of that particular task is becoming apparent, and it looks as if the brushtail possum, *Trichosurus vulpecula*, will be with us for a long time to come.

Seventy million possums—20 per man, woman and child living in the country. That's the current estimate of the possum population, and, in spite of vigorous control programmes, the figure seems to be remaining stable.

These 70 million pairs of jaws consume something like 21,000 tonnes of green matter every 24 hours—the equivalent of a big container ship full of leaves, young shoots, berries, flowers and grasses departing from our shores every night.

No forest can be expected to sustain such depletion for long, and our trees have been giving up the ghost in a big way for at least 50 years. Ironically, in the early part of this century very few people considered the possum to be anything but an asset. The prevailing opinion was succinctly voiced by the Auckland Acclimatisation Society, one of many groups charged with introducing beneficial species into what, to Victorian eyes, looked like a bland and empty landscape. Said the Society in a 1917 report: "We shall be doing a great service to the country in stocking these large areas [of rough bush] with this valuable and harmless animal."

Such was the government's concern for the welfare of the little Australian newcomer that the possum was given various levels of legal protection from 1889 until 1947. However, right from the start possums sparked controversy. Orchardists, who were already experiencing the effects of the possum's big appetite in the 1880s, demanded that protection be removed; so did possum trappers, who wanted open slather. Acclimatisation societies, on the other hand, pressured government to retain protection of what they regarded as a valuable resource.

So, in 1911, protection was increased. In 1912, it was withdrawn. In 1913, it was back in place. It wasn't until the

KENNEDY WARNE

Death by possum has been the fate of forests throughout the country, but nowhere is it more graphic than on Northland's coast, where the skeletons of pohutukawa stand out starkly on the ridges.

1940s that the public began to see the possum's "great service" had turned into a full-grown threat. Even then, the primary reason for wanting to curb the population was the damage possums did to orchards and erosion control plantings, and their propensity for climbing power poles and shorting out the wires. Right up until the middle of this century it was claimed that possum damage to forests was negligible compared to the benefits of the fur trade.

All this time, while the government was see-sawing on the possum question, legal (up to 1922) and then illegal liberations of possums continued up and down the country. The trapper's mind, honed by a century of colonial prejudice, could see no reason why New Zealand's "empty" bush—all it contained were a few birds and the occasional weta—shouldn't provide him with a living from fur.

That mentality persists to the present day. As recently as the mid-1980s possums were deliberately released into the Far North, and by 1989 they had reached Cape Reinga.

Possums have the country covered, and the Department of Conservation (DOC), which has most of New Zealand's best stands of native forest in its charge, is tearing its corporate hair out trying to control them. DOC gave up on an all-out assault mentality some years ago. Neil Clifton, a conservation officer on the South Island's West Coast, where 75 per cent of the rata-kamahi forests have suffered severe possum damage, says, "You could throw the government's entire budget at possums and still not win. They have spread across too wide a front for us to be able to hold them. All we can do is pick a number of 'islands'—areas we think we can defend—and then try to preserve them."

Around the country, DOC offices have been drawing up their own lists of "islands." One of them is the tip of the Coromandel Peninsula, from Colville Bay north, incorporating Mt Moehau, an area with a unique native fauna and flora that includes two rare frogs, the North Island kaka and the North Island brown kiwi.

Because the Moehau region is surrounded by sea on three

After spending the first few months of its life in its mother's pouch, the joey hitches a free ride on her back until it is ready to face the world on its own.

sides and connected to the rest of the Coromandel Peninsula by a relatively narrow isthmus (about five kilometres across) DOC plans to build an electrified fence across the peninsula, then use intensive hunting and trapping techniques to eliminate all possums north of the fence.

Being German, I can't help but be reminded of the Berlin Wall, with our "Checkpoint Charlie" being just north of Colville. Yet the same system that kept the East Germans in might keep the possums out, in which case it would be one of the few victories in an ongoing battle to save our forests.

So far, the only places where possums have been completely eradicated have been actual islands, including Codfish, near Stewart Island, Kapiti, north-west of Wellington, and Rangitoto, in Auckland's Hauraki Gulf.

It took six years to destroy Kapiti's 20,000 possums, but the results have been startling. Possum removal has led to a renaissance in vegetation—especially of the highly possum-palatable plants such as fuchsia, toro and kohekohe. In the case of kohekohe, surveys estimate up to a million new seedlings per hectare. Previously, these trees had been prevented from flowering by possums browsing the buds.

Bird numbers have also increased. Not only do possums deprive birds of berries, nectar and some insects, but they compete for nest sites in hollow trees, and have even been observed to devour young birds and eggs. (As one scientist remarked, "It could be expected that an animal endowed with teeth and curiosity sufficient to induce it to open sealed tins of condensed milk would not be averse to sampling any other unusual object encountered.")

By comparison with islands, mainland forests are much more difficult sites for possum eradication because of the problem of reinvasion. In these forests, an initial kill, no matter how successful, must be followed up by regular maintenance control to prevent a new population from establishing itself in the possum-free area.

Although it is now well known that possums kill trees by defoliating them, their cumulative effect on our vegetation is more subtle and pervasive. Possums are picky eaters with definite dietary preferences. At any one time, some half-dozen plant species will constitute 75 per cent of a possum's diet.

Possums are quite happy with introduced tree fodder as well as native species, including pines (they go for the pollen-bearing catkins and strip the bark to get at the sweet tissues underneath), orchard fruit and erosion control trees such as poplars.

The problem with possum browsing is not just what they eat, but also how they eat. Possums will return night after night to a single tree, systematically stripping it before moving on to another of the same species. No one is sure of the reason for this behaviour, but the effect is to give the tree no chance to regenerate after each night's onslaught.

Despite efforts by concerned groups to replant affected

DAVID MATHIESON

Possums are not often seen during the day; they are usually asleep in their dens, located in a hollow log or in the fork of a tree.

areas, most forest ecologists are pessimistic about the future of our native bush. Although possums have been with us for 150 years, nowhere in New Zealand have they and the forest yet reached an equilibrium. Forests continue to be downgraded as larger tree species are browsed to death, to be replaced by scrub, grasses and gorse. If the trend continues, then forests will end up being full of species unpalatable to possums, and the New Zealand bush will be a sickly and uninviting shadow of its former self.

Of even greater concern is the fact that possums spread bovine tuberculosis, and could potentially put at risk the core of New Zealand's export trade: our meat and dairy products.

Tonight, three of us are out to do some spotlighting. I have selected an area that has been trapped previously, and the spotlight is to give us a better idea of the numbers of possums left. It is a calm, warm night, and a good cover of clouds disguises the light of the moon. The little beam of my torch throws out just enough light to show us our way.

Suddenly, a noise. Something is running up a tree. We all stop in our tracks. I switch on the powerful spotlight. Mounted underneath the barrel of the rifle, a .22 magnum, the beam is instantly probing the spot where the noise was last heard. A big grey trunk is all we can see.

"That fellow must have had a bad encounter with a spotlight before," someone remarks. True, possums do get spotlight-shy. For an animal that's half a sandwich short of a picnic, they learn remarkably fast.

A big moth is attracted by the light, and casts eerie shadows on the trees. Suddenly, out of nowhere, completely silent, a morepork darts through the night, catches the moth and disappears, leaving behind a startled bunch of great white hunters.

After we compose ourselves, I shine the light into the branches of the old puriri again, and there it is. Stunned by the bright beam, the possum looks straight down the barrel. I bring the rifle up to my shoulder, take aim and pull the trigger. The animal hits the ground with a thump. We walk over to examine the carcass. It's a big grey female, so routinely I check the pouch for young. In the north, with its warmer climate, abundant food supply and lower possum density, as many as 80 per cent of the females breed twice a year. In optimum conditions, a female joey can virtually step off its mother's back at seven months and fall pregnant a couple of months later. Whether its offspring survives, however, depends on the population density and the carrying capacity of the forest.

In the Orongorongo Valley, east of Wellington, live the most-studied possums in the country. Scientists from the nearby land resources division of the Department of Scientific and Industrial Research have been trapping, tagging, radio-tracking and otherwise monitoring this population for 25 years, and have built up a revealing picture of possum population dynamics based on this work.

It is the females who run the place, says Bob Brockie, one of the senior possum scientists at the DSIR. They control the home ranges, and hand them down from mother to daughter. Sons are usually forced to leave and look for a new home range. The net result is that the core population consists largely of groups of related females, with the males dispersing outwards. If the carrying capacity of the forest has been reached, then no new home ranges will be available, and many offspring will die during the winter.

New Zealand possums are a pretty unsociable lot. Apart from the occasional hissing, paw-slashing scrap when animals cross paths, each individual keeps to itself for most of the year. The exception is during the mating season, when young bucks will be competing for available females. At this time of year you can often find cottonball-sized fluffs of fur in the bush— evidence both of increased contact between males and failed attempts to approach females which are not in oestrus.

While possums generally go out of their way to avoid each other, they have no interest in defending a large territory for the sake of it. They do, however, advertise their presence by rubbing trees with their scent glands.

Australian brushtail possums are more territorial than their New Zealand counterparts, a fact that is attributed to scarcity of den sites, the more open nature of the eucalypt forest in which they live, and the lower nutritional value of Australian vegetation. To a species which had adapted to such conditions, New Zealand's dense, lush forest, with den sites aplenty and a veritable smorgasbord of plant matter, must have seemed like possum heaven, and the animal's territorial instincts probably collapsed under the pressure of numbers.

The brushtail possum is only one of 20 or more possum species in Australia, but it is the most common, and one of the largest. Aboriginal legend connects the possum to the man in the moon. Once upon a time, so the story goes, Moonan, a warrior, and his sons went hunting for witchetty grubs. The moon shone bright in the night sky, and they soon came across a big tree where they hoped to find many grubs. Moonan climbed to the top of the tree, and to his great joy found that he could reach the moon.

As his sons rocked the tree in their excitement, he nearly fell out of the branches, and to save himself he clambered on to the moon. The sons quickly climbed the tree after him, but by the time they reached the top the moon had drifted away.

Ever since, when the moon is bright, the sons climb trees to find their father. Through the ages they have grown sharp claws on their fingers, and a long tail from their spine. They have become possums.

Perhaps the story needs a New Zealand ending, I wonder, as I walk along the forest track under my own moonlit sky, spotlight at the ready. One where Moonan comes back to earth, finds out what his sons have done, and shoots every last one of them.

A familiar sight on virtually any back country road in New Zealand: a possum about to become a statistic. For most people, it is difficult to be upset by the death of animals which in other circumstances could be regarded as ideal pets. With forest destruction all around, it's a case of the possums or the trees.

From icebergs to breadfruit trees

MARK SCOTT

M/V Gondwana, *one of Greenpeace's fleet, shoulders aside pack ice on a voyage to Ross Dependency, the New Zealand-administered slice of Antarctica. In winter, ice forms an unbroken sheet extending 1500 km offshore.*

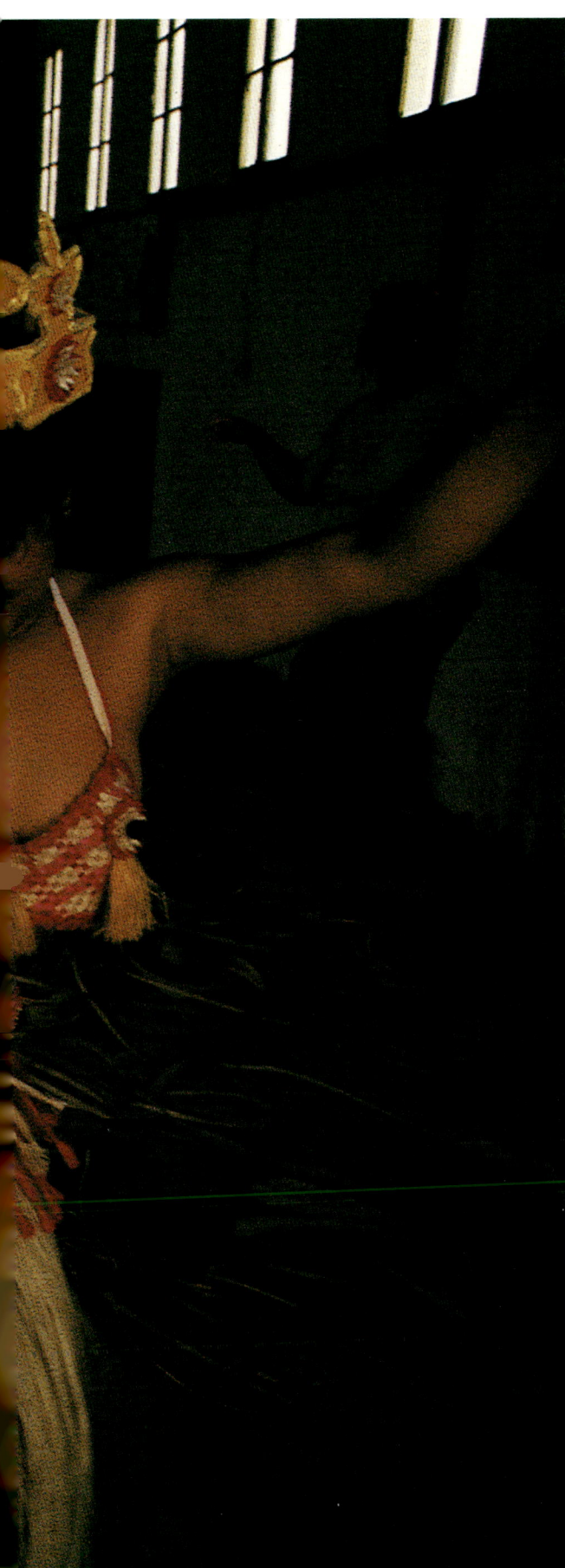

W hen it became apparent early in 1995 that New Zealand was going to trounce *Stars and Stripes* and carry off the America's Cup, the world media inevitably began to ask: what, if not where, is New Zealand? And how was it that a pipsqueak country of three million people could outsail and outsmart the land that gave us McDonald's and *Baywatch*.

How indeed, as one reporter mused, when the only thing New Zealand has more of than the United States is sheep droppings.

That we are small and remote and have dirt on our gumboots is a fact New Zealanders understand all too well. Even by jumbo jet, it takes a long time to get to anywhere of significance from here. On the scale of the world's great continents and their populations measured in hundreds of millions, we are a shag on a rock, gazing wistfully at an empty horizon.

That New Zealand is not without its own modest "empire"—one that stretches from the South Pole to just shy of the Equator—is a fact less well understood. True, the land area is of little consequence, but the geographical spread is impressive: 8000 kilometres from icebergs to coral atolls, penguins to breadfruit trees. And all of it part and parcel of New Zealand.

Southernmost of these territories is Ross Dependency, a wedge of Antarctica which takes in McMurdo Sound and the Ross Ice Shelf, and is rich in the history of Antarctic exploration. New Zealand operates a year-round research centre there, at Scott Base, where scientists examine everything from the natural antifreeze in Antarctic fish blood to the hole in the ozone layer.

Between latitudes 50 and 60 South—a belt of the Southern Ocean known as the "Furious Fifties"—lie a cluster of small uninhabited islands which boast some of the largest seabird colonies in the world, as well as prodigious numbers of marine mammals and spectacular plants called megaherbs. It has been said that more seabirds nest on the Bounty Islands, with a land area of just one square kilometre, than in the whole of Great Britain.

Until 1995, Campbell Island, site of the "loneliest tree on Earth" (see story beginning

ARNO GASTEIGER

Skilled hands turn pandanus into colourful garments at a women's craft collective on Mauke in the southern Cook Islands. When the time comes to try the fit, hands and hips just can't keep from swaying.

page 184) was also home to a handful of meteorologists and biologists who recorded the perturbations of its weather and the fortunes of its wildlife. Now the only human presence to disturb the albatrosses and elephant seals is the occasional party of ecotourists dropping anchor in Perseverance Harbour.

Roughly as far north of New Zealand as Campbell is south of it lie the Kermadecs, a group of volcanoes which link geologically to the thermal regions of Rotorua and White Island and are part of the Pacific Ring of Fire. The largest, Raoul Island, has a resident crew of weather and wildlife people who enjoy somewhat balmier—if also riskier—conditions than their erstwhile counterparts in the subantarctic. In 1993, the team had to be hastily evacuated when Raoul threatened to erupt.

As well as being wildlife sanctuaries, the Kermadec Islands have recently become the site of one of the world's largest marine reserves. Giant limpets, huge grouper, strange sea whips and colourful soft corals—components of a marine ecosystem that is unique among the world's oceans—are the beneficiaries.

Sail north from Raoul Island for about 2500 kilometres, walk out along the palm-fringed coral reef of Atafu, one of the three atolls of the Tokelau group, and you will eventually stand at the northernmost tip of *terra aotearoa*. Tokelau is New Zealand's last Pacific dependency. Prior to their gaining independence, Niue, Western Samoa and the Cook Islands were also administered by New Zealand.

These and other islands of the western Pacific remain strongly linked with New Zealand. (Indeed, more Niueans and Tokelauans live here than in their home islands.) And the Polynesian presence in New Zealand has encouraged the country as a whole to see itself less as an outpost of Europe—the old colonial idea of being the sheep farm, cheese factory and sawmill of England—and more as a partner in the Pacific.

It's a shift in thinking that *New Zealand Geographic* has tried to promote. Feature articles on Tokelau and the Cook Islands have shown that all is not kava and cricket on these islands where the wheels of progress can grind heavily against traditions maintained in isolation for countless generations. Forget Club Med and images of happy natives dancing their lives away. Most Pacific nations are in a complex political and administrative stew of questions about trade, education, decolonisation, social hierarchies and resource management.

So too on the Chathams—islands to the east of New Zealand where calls for greater autonomy have grown increasingly strident in recent years. The magazine's portrayal of life on these island associates, together with coverage of the natural and human history of the Kermadecs, Campbell Island, the Auckland Islands and Ross Dependency, has, we hope, meant that the word "New Zealand" now has a little more breadth than it did before.

ARNO GASTEIGER

Chatham Islands priest and flounder fisher Riwai Preece will share his catch even with those who don't attend his sermons. Remoteness breeds self-reliance and a gritty comradeship among the islands' 750 inhabitants.

GLENN JOWITT

Thick plaster walls (to keep out the heat), gothic windows, bright splashes of colour and an elaborate "wedding-cake" pulpit mark this sanctuary in Manihiki Atoll as belonging to the Cook Islands Christian Church.

ARNO GASTEIGER

Fifteen tiny islands and atolls strewn across close to a million square miles of ocean, the Cooks are the very definition of isolation. A weekly air service eases the remoteness for the inhabitants of many islands, including Mangaia.

KIM WESTERSKOV

Lone Adélie penguin makes the long march to its rookery near Scott Base, McMurdo Sound, where New Zealand has a research centre. Adélies often walk tens of kilometres across the ice on their daily journeys to and from the sea.

ROGER GRACE

Galapagos shark glides past a school of demoiselle, whose white spots gleam like eyes against the inky blue water of the Kermadecs. A 7350-square kilometre marine reserve protects the subtropical species found around these islands.

following pages: KENNEDY WARNE

Whatever they do, whether taro planting or hymn singing (as here, at a village choir competition celebrating the coming of the Gospel to the island of Aitutaki), Cook Islanders do it with verve and humour.

ARNO GASTEIGER

The 44 South Motor Cycle Club claims that there are more Harley-Davidsons per head on Chatham Island than anywhere else in the world. The "hogs" are hard to keep clean: there are virtually no sealed roads on the island.

ARNO GASTEIGER

Today, Rarotonga's children complain if they don't get jam and butter on their bread; ten years ago, the loaf itself was the luxury. Such incidental contrasts underline the changes which are occurring in many Pacific societies.

following pages: KIM WESTERSKOV

Defying massive surf on the west coast of the main Auckland Island, a light-mantled sooty albatross skims the ocean in search of food. The bird's 2.5-metre wingspan gives some idea of the size of the waves.

Tokelau

By MARK SCOTT
Photographs by ARNO GASTEIGER

Abridged from New Zealand Geographic, *October - December, 1994*

IN SOME WAYS, Tokelau is even more isolated than Antarctica, where the New Zealand flag flies over our only other dependency. Every summer, RNZAF Hercules aircraft rumble back and forth to McMurdo Sound, but no plane disturbs the silence of this threadbare necklace of atolls north of Samoa, because there's no airstrip. The only way in and out is by tramp steamer that calls from Apia, stopping only briefly. You could be stranded for months. Until this year, there wasn't even a telephone.

There are few countries left in the Pacific where the weekly plane-load of tourists and the wage packet haven't undermined the authority of the traditional order. But on Tokelau, so I learned from the few books that have been written about the place, the minutiae of daily life are still strictly ordered by councils of elders that direct the menfolk when to work the village gardens, when to fish and how the catch is to be divided among the households of the village. I learned that on these smatterings of pure coral rock the bare business of gathering or growing enough food requires an interdependence that is held together by a disciplined hierarchy of rules, tuned by tradition—still largely intact.

In 1994, a chance overlap in shipping allowed *New Zealand Geographic* photographer Arno Gasteiger and me to travel to Tokelau with a reasonable certainty of getting off again. We hitched a lift to the middle atoll, Nukunonu, with the navy survey ship *Monowai*. There a survey team had been checking tide levels, to better predict the effects of global warming, rising oceans and whether or not there'd even be a Tokelau in a hundred years' time.

Our visit coincided with a fact-finding mission from the United Nations. For years, the UN has been encouraging Tokelau towards independence, while for their part the islanders steadfastly refuse to sever links with New Zealand, although they have gained more say in the running of their own affairs.

New Zealand inherited from Britain in 1925 the responsibility for administering Tokelau. Then we treated Tokelau as a distant and forgotten outpost of Samoa, which was already the victim of shameful and brutal mismanagement by New Zealand colonial officials. In 1948, Tokelau was incorporated as part of New Zealand,

Homesickness and uncertainty show on the faces of Tokelauans returning to their islands—New Zealand's last Pacific dependency.

Nukunonu, like Tokelau's two other atolls, consists of a ribbon of coral rock fringing a huge lagoon. Together, the atolls boast a land area of just 12 square kilometres. Should the sea level rise, much of that land would be swamped.

with its affairs being run from a desk in Wellington.

Now, in response to demands from Tokelau, the public service is shifting to the actual atolls it is supposed to be administering. Not only that, but the service will be run by Tokelauans.

Landfall, by rights, should have been by traditional longboat, but photographer Arno Gasteiger and I flew ashore by navy helicopter. From the air, Nukunonu's lagoon shone like an extraordinary opal shot with flecked turquoises that shifted in the play of sunlight. Around the edges of this impossible jewel clung a narrow crust of coral that sprouted coconut palms and, on one island, a shore-to-shore clutter of fibrolite, Cooper louvre windows and corrugated iron.

The chopper set us down at the school. No child showed a face at a class window. No adult appeared. But, after walking some distance, we located the store, always a focal point on islands like these: a place to wait for the world to go by so that you can watch it when it does. A dozen eyes swivelled in our direction.

"Hello, we're from the *New Zealand Geographic* magazine. It's good to be here at last. Does anyone know where the EO is? I think somebody radioed to tell him we were coming."

One of the men, with a shift of the eyebrows, indicated that maybe, just maybe, he was the Executive Officer, the man I was seeking. A pained silence followed. His face creased with botherment. "Got any hostuff?" he eventually whispered. *Pardon me?* "Got any hostuff? We haven't had a ship for months."

After a deal of trial and error I determined the EO was speaking to his thirst, "hostuff" being the local name for spirits—hot stuff as opposed to cold stuff, for which he was also desperate. "We've run out of beer. We've had no beer for two months. No beer, no hostuff—and we've got a disco tonight. Can you sell us some beer?" This was a predicament I was unable to assuage—least of all with the bottle of brandy packed in my bag.

Rampant hostuff and disco on this step-back-in-time unspoiled island paradise? "Oh, yes. We have disco all the time—in the cargo shed. Fund-raisers. We drink *kaleve* we make from the coconut tree, but tonight's disco is special. It's to say goodbye to the navy boys."

I suggested he buy his supplies from *Monowai*, where, from entirely casual observation, there had appeared to be no shortage of liquids. The shelves of Nukunonu's store, on the other hand, were virtually bare. The island was down to its last cans of bully beef, packets of ship's biscuits, its last few pairs of jandals. Since we weren't in need of jandals there wasn't a lot of choice, but, even so, our purchases were overseen by three employees.

"A can of beef and a packet of biscuits," I asked the woman behind the polished hardboard counter. This she communicated to an assistant standing beside her. His speciality, obvi-

ously, was to locate items on the shelves. The shop manager, installed in a booth, recorded the transaction.

Later that night a general crunching of footfalls along the coral paths leading to the cargo shed indicated the disco was about to begin. In the cool night air, with a huge moon spreading pools of light across an endless ocean, the fussy floral fragrance of the women's perfume gathered strength, mixing with the clove tang of brilliantine.

Inside, grandfathers tangoed with granddaughters, and grandmothers loud with flirtatious merriment hauled sailors out on to the dance floor. To the beat of the music (and the portable generator—the island's main generator had been out of order for months) Nukunonu partied on down. The entire island—minus the infants and press-ganged baby-sitters—seemed to have turned out.

This was disco closer to a backblocks Kiwi woolshed "do" than anything out of New York. The shed was decorated with

coconut palm fronds, coloured lights were strung from the ceiling, and at intervals during the night the school principal dispensed bottles of hostuff as prizes—from a stash he'd somehow kept the EO out of. A bottle of Vat 69 for the best dancing. A bourbon or two for the best-dressed couples.

At midnight sharp the sound system was unplugged, a hymn and concluding prayer offered and the disco mamas and papas of Nukunonu strolled the few short steps home.

Arno and I both woke with splitting hostuff headaches, which pain a breakfast of ship's biscuit, bully beef and a cup of

Spear-wielding diver "moon-walks" across the coral at Atafu, northernmost of the three atolls which make up Tokelau. His catch of colourful reef-hugging fish will supplement the catch of ocean species such as tuna.

brackish tank-water did little to remedy. We also woke to the moment I'd been waiting for: the savour of total isolation. With the navy gone there was now literally no way of getting off this island. It was a feeling I had come a long way for.

First stop was the local school to talk to Luciano Perez, the principal and, as I had discovered the previous evening, the organiser of Nukunonu's discos. As I waited for him, I studied the library. You can tell a lot about a school by its library, and the shelves in Luciano's were well stocked. On the wall were children's posters that cheerily encouraged reading. Children fishing for books, cuddling books. "Hook a book! Hug a book!"

You can also tell a lot about a school by whether or not the children are treated as adults. As I spoke to Luciano there were constant requests for attention from well-mannered children who approached in total confidence. They won Luciano's instant unfussed focus. I complimented him on his pupils'

Children walk the coral rock walls of the communal piggery on Atafu. Each family has its own pen, and is responsible for the care of its own animals. Pork and poultry are the main sources of non-fish protein in Tokelau.

easy confidence.

"Yes, yes, I like to see them like that. It's not the Tokelau way, not *faka* Tokelau—that way children are supposed to stay very quiet and not to think for themselves. Hah! The old people always spend their time preaching at the children to stop doing things. I spend my time preaching at them to *do* things. You don't want to stop their brain developing.

"Skateboards—they wanted to stop them. Children were breaking bones. But I say, let them break their bones—that's their way of reaching for the sky. If we stop their interests they

might stop being interested in anything. Where does that leave children? They wanted them to be happy whipping a hoop, like they did. Hah! Faka Tokelau—the Tokelau way—has to learn about change.

"The old people misjudge the young generation. There is too much for them to understand. They say too much talk from the young people is dangerous. Now we have money, outboard motors, compost—" *Compost?* "Yes, compost. We talk about the environment, we have how many posters, but still the people burn all the leaves. Brainless! It's all been explained how the plants rely on each other and need compost, but it takes a long time for people to understand change."

Luciano moves from compost to commerce. "There's a lot of talk about sustained autonomy and not relying on hand-outs. Try small business development, they tell us. Start a bakery, do sewing, raise poultry. But sustained autonomy needs new discipline. If you pay someone to be a nurse, then she should be at the hospital, not at someone's house drinking kaleve when you need her.

"The people in the Apia office that administers our islands are even worse in their attitude. We depend on them to order goods for us. You send the money, but when the ship comes there's no goods and no money. So you radio the office and they tell you, "Sorry, we lost your money," and you can't force any action. There's nobody to turn to. They haven't stolen your money, they've just spent it. Faka Tokelau makes people very casual about these things: there's always fish in the sea and breadfruit up the tree, and it belongs to the village, to everyone.

"Our inati system of sharing is really disturbed by money. Before, you give everything to the village and the village gives you back your share—fish, bananas, taro. But nobody gives their wages to the village. Those with jobs still get their share of the food, but don't do the work to gather it. This causes jealousy."

I want to know how New Zealand has performed in its least-known backwater. "New Zealand has not taken its responsibilities very seriously. They didn't even have a proper school here until the 1950s. When it opened, the old people came along too, to learn how to read and write. How can you talk about sustained autonomy when education is so new? You need to educate many generations before you can educate a society." Luciano shakes his head at the waste of potential.

Strolling off to the store to lay in a decent supply of bully beef and crackers (the cargo ship isn't due for at least a week), I discover our morning of isolation is at an end. Tokelau's inter-atoll ferry, a tubby steel catamaran, has arrived over-night to take *Monowai*'s place.

This is surprising. Innumerable phone calls from New Zealand to the Tokelau office in Apia about the logistics of internal travel had earlier failed to reveal this ship's existence.

The essence of these tiny islands is an ineffable cooperation. Mundane tasks are sweetened by the rhythms of song and the bonds of companionship in communities of just a few hundred people. On a picnic to a remote islet, one woman kneads, another strums, another keeps time, another waves away flies.

Its appearance means that Arno and I can now visit the northern atoll of Atafu, rumoured to be Tokelau's most beautiful and the most traditionally-minded.

We take the boat that night and wake to find ourselves already anchored off the reef at Atafu. Around the boat are a handful of outrigger canoes, powered by outboards. In the deep blue, almost purple, waters, fishermen are diving for the day's bait. They use small fishing rods to cast their lines while they dive. Because the fishermen are in the water with the fish, they're able to steer the baited hook directly to the target, and see when it bites. On Tokelau there is nothing unusual about the sight of men catching fish, but everybody's watching all the same. There is no tiring of the magic of hauling livelihood from the sea.

At the canoe landing the elders have a shed for playing cards, carving and generally shooting the breeze. It's also the place where the fishermen's catch is divided among the village. This way of sharing is called inati, and the slicing up of the great barrel-chested tuna is a precision business attended by an elder who calculates the need of each household according to the age and number in it.

The children who are allotted the job of sizing the fish reward themselves by reaching between the gills and pulling out some prized organ they chew raw. On Tokelau there's none of the palagi reluctance to partake of raw fish. Fishermen think nothing of tearing tuna to pieces with their teeth. Children will clutch fish streaming blood and slime as if they were teddy bears. I saw one child wearing the head of a huge tuna as a mask.

Across from the inati landing in the elders' hut the carvers work, adzing fishing tackle boxes from Atafu's famed varie-gated kanava hardwood. I'm not the only one sitting awhile, watching on. Some play cards. One snoozes, a wooden pillow tucked in the nape of his neck. These elder craftsmen some-how splay their feet out in front of them, using the upturned soles as a cushioned workbench, the upholstery of flesh preventing the finely detailed wood from splitting under the adze blows.

One master carver, wearing patched spectacle frames with lenses that could have been cut from the base of a Coke bottle, is detailing a rebate that takes the lid: endless paring blows that see the wood fall away like shavings of milk chocolate. *Tok tok tok.* Where any Kiwi chippie would be figuring out how to get a band-saw in on the act, these men seem to prolong the act of creating.

The last of the children sent for the inati share stagger off up the path clutching armfuls of tuna. A truck trundles by with banana leaves for compost. Not *a* truck, *the* truck. A child husks coconut on a spear. Someone carts a load of sand somewhere, the bucket swinging from a notched carry-stick lying across his shoulder. The carver sheaths his adze in a coconut husk and chews a chunk of fish. The shopkeeper lady

Every afternoon, when the heat goes out of the day, Nukunonu's young people gather at the Catholic Church for volleyball. They play until dark, when a curfew dictates that they must return to their homes.

walks by, swinging a bunch of keys with a certain ostentation on an island where there are few locks.

The apparently well-balanced calm of a society ordered by established rituals and hierarchies doesn't wash with many of the younger folk. "This is a very small island, but they have a hundred thousand rules," one woman explained. "No cards on Sunday, women can't drink, you can't travel across the lagoon without permission. I respect what I know is right, but why should a man drink when his wife can't?"

During a netball game at Atafu school, I ask a player how she sees Tokelau's future. "You're looking at it. What it is now is what it'll always be. The be all and end all is that the old men try to control everything, and until they take off somewhere . . . I don't know . . . take them to visit the 20th century . . . then this place won't get anywhere. That's because no-one with hopes and expectations is willing to put up with all the meddling in your life."

Tokelau's population is remarkably stable. In 1963, New Zealand provided assisted immigration to ease overcrowding, but the scheme was halted in 1976. Between then and now the population has stayed at around 1600—this despite the free access to New Zealand that has denuded Niue and parts of the Cook Islands.

Many leave Tokelau for schooling, jobs and family reasons—some 4000 Tokelauans live in New Zealand—but just as many return.

How difficult is coming back? I talked to Mena Moti, a young married woman trying hard to adjust to a very different life. "There's no question about it, it's hard here. Nothing happens. Nothing changes. You have to keep yourself occupied somehow to keep sane . . . Well, you are occupied. There's no escape from it. It's a constant battle to keep this hut tidy . . . there's the dust, the sand, the chooks . . . you sweep a thousand times a day, you do your washing in a bucket, you cook on a fire, and what's there to cook? Fish, rice, breadfruit, coconut. Fish, rice, breadfruit, coconut."

On Tokelau, women very seldom get to leave the confines of even the home island—not to zoom out across the reef in an outboard dinghy to the open spaces of the ocean to fish, nor to cross the lagoon to the gardens on other islands, nor to experience the extraordinary universe that lies under the water. All these areas are preserves for men. It is the unusually bold woman that enters them. Certainly, no mother has the time.

Until this year, the day-to-day business of Tokelau was administered from an office in Apia, with a large slice of the budget being spent in Samoa rather than Tokelau. The reason? Lack of a telephone and a boat meant that it was impossible to administer Tokelau from any of the atolls. The purchase of a small catamaran and the installation of a single telephone on each of the islands has now allowed the office (and its budget) to shift to Tokelau.

Supping beer on a verandah, I speak to a young Tokelauan who is in Fakaofo, the third and most populous atoll, to install Tokelau's first telephone. "So Tokelau's about to see some changes," I prompt him.

"No, just because we have a telephone doesn't mean Tokelau wants change. We don't want development here. What else is there except for tourism? Outsiders paying us to do our dances? Everywhere I go I see the more developed a place is, the more unequal it is. In our custom everything is equal, but if I get a good job and my cousin doesn't then that's not equal any more. I get richer and richer and he gets worse and worse.

"Good old New Zealand hasn't done much, but at least they've left us alone. We wouldn't be better off under the French. They'd be cutting a channel through the atoll, building a port for the big ships. We don't want that. We prefer to mess around in our little boats, dropping everything in the surf. They'd have tourists here, a Club Med. There'd be French schools. We're lucky New Zealand's done nothing!"

Eliu Iosua, a school teacher, confirms the feeling. "Life here is completely satisfying. The losses of the 20th century are heavier than the gains. We don't need all that stuff here. There's no other people like us in the whole world. Why should we trade that for a hotel or an airport?"

In my last days at Fakaofo, without realising it, I am quietly absorbed into a community of perhaps 600 people living on an island no bigger than a few football fields. I stroll the narrow lanes crowded by a huddle of houses, listening to the school playground intensity of chatter. I'm invited into homes where I learn of the daily struggles and the hopes for the future. I bathe under a tap twice a day. I listen to the guttural calls of the town crier doing his rounds. All of this means nothing in particular, but all of it adds up to Tokelau.

I recall a conversation I had with a young Tokelauan visiting Tokelau for the first time. John Taupe, who back in New Zealand worked at a Hutt Valley K Mart, was steering a dinghy at midnight across the lagoon at Fakaofo when we talked of why Tokelau holds such a powerful attraction.

As we slipped across the waters, the unbelievably twinkling stars were reflected in the steel calm of the lagoon. Beyond the reef the swell of the endless ocean crashed and spumed a frothy white in the moonlight.

John turned and said, "You know, my grandfather had a dying wish. He told me about the home star, the home star that guided his canoe from Fakaofo here, all the way home to Atafu. He described that star to me, took a lot of trouble to tell me about that star, but I was young and I was in New Zealand and had no interest. It meant nothing to me. Now I'm here under all these stars, and I don't really know which one it is. Now that I want to know, I don't know. His dying wish was for me to come home to Tokelau, to come back to his home. To find the star. So I am here."

Tranquil evening scene belies a sense of unease experienced by many islanders. Increasingly, they are being asked to choose between the promises of development and the security of traditional ways. So far, most prefer change to come slowly, if at all. "Our isolation is our strength," they say.

Campbell

By RAEWYN MACKENZIE

Abridged from New Zealand Geographic, *January - March, 1989*

THE WATCHERS HAVE ALREADY been up for hours by the time the *Daniel Solander* pulls into Perseverance Harbour at 5.45 A.M.

As we come into sight of their settlement we can see them through the drizzling rain standing at the window of their dimly-lit accommodation quarters, watching the arrival of the first outside people they have seen in eight months. This is the ship which will take them back to New Zealand after a year on New Zealand's southernmost meteorological station.

On board is the replacement crew. They will spend a year here, observing and recording the weather patterns across the grim Southern Ocean. All first-timers except for their leader, Paul Hatfield, they have been well prepared for this sight: the rocky, tussocked hills flanking the harbour, the utilitarian buildings of the weather station huddling under Beeman Hill. But they, too, are subdued as the ship drops anchor a couple of hundred metres across the water from their new home. The temperature is 7.3 degrees, the wind chill factor reducing it to about zero.

Back out towards the harbour entrance the wind is tearing chunks of the water into wild, spinning loops that dance across the surface. Giant petrels, huge dark birds, wheel slowly overhead, and, 50 metres away, oblivious to the ship's presence, young sea lions are playing in the kelp.

Lying 600 km south of Stewart Island, Campbell Island is southernmost of a scattering of islands which include the Bounty Islands, the Antipodes, the Snares and the Auckland Islands—all under New Zealand control. It is hammered by gale-force winds for much of the time and receives an average of 653 hours of sunshine each year (contrast that with Invercargill's 1600 hours), with less than one hour of sunshine a day for 215 days of the year. There is not much difference between winter and summer temperatures— the mean is six degrees.

Most of New Zealand's weather comes from the west and the south, and Campbell Island lies right in its path. This makes it one of the most important weather stations in New Zealand.

Given the gloominess of the weather, you would wonder how

SCOTT FREEMAN

Snow can fall in any month of the year at bleak, mountainous Campbell Island, one of several subantarctic islands administered by New Zealand.

the Meteorological Service could find anyone to go there, but almost all of this year's team have applied more than once to go down.

On board ship there's a delay while people eat breakfast, stocking up for a day's work unloading and reloading the ship with the tonnes of equipment needed for a remote post. There's food enough for a year, replacement machinery, drums of caustic soda and sacks of aluminium filings to make the hydrogen for the weather balloons. There's a cage of hens with one rooster which has been crowing his heart out for two hours, and 250 dozen beer the new team has brought in to while away the long, long winter nights.

Today the sun has come out. It spreads over Mt Honey, across the harbour from the base, and the craggy hills are softened by its peach-yellow light into pinks and browns and

ROGER MOFFAT

Jagged-leafed megaherbs of the carrot family and purple-flowered giant daisies form a lush and colourful ground cover on many parts of Campbell Island.

greens. I get a glimmer of the spell which has made Hatfield say that for him, coming back to Campbell is "like a home-coming."

The crew at Beeman Base live a spartan but comfortable life. Buildings are set widely apart in case of fire. Skuas, large brown gull-like birds ("with disgusting eating habits," says one of the departing team) are tame as household cats, strolling around our feet as we stand outside talking.

Books come from the National Library service, and there is a video player, film projector, gym equipment, pool table and

dartboard. Over the past year the crew has been taking part in an Antarctic/subantarctic darts tournament.

"During a radio schedule one day, Scott Base suggested we play darts with them," says Rob Crawley, technician for the departing team. "We'd throw, tell each other our scores and write it up on the blackboards." Eventually the tournament extended to nearby Macquarie Island and Casey (one of the two Australian bases on Antarctica) and the Greenpeace Antarctic base.

For some, the year on Campbell is a chance for self-improvement. This year Richard Ward has taken French records to improve his ability to speak the language of his wife Aline, whom he married two weeks before this trip. Gerald Hamilton has brought maths and physics books to help with future engineering study.

The isolation is not absolute. They will have radio phone contact with the mainland, and there should be at least two mail drops by air force Orions, but with winds gusting up to over 100 knots these often have to be called off.

When the mail does arrive, there's an instant holiday.

Only serious health problems get them a trip home. Wendy Strid, the cook leaving the island, was here the previous year, too, until she broke her leg and a Japanese trawler had to be diverted to take her to Dunedin.

Paul Hatfield, as officer in charge of the base, will have to sort out the inevitable friction which happens in a close-knit group. People run out of things to say to each other, get bored and become depressed by the long hours of darkness—from 4.30 P.M. to 9 A.M. in winter.

"It's usually the small niggling things which cause the tension," Hatfield says. "Things like whether you eat noisily, whether someone wears their boots inside the hostel, smoking while someone's eating."

Biologist Peter Moore tells me that what he has noticed most is the amount of recreation time he has on his hands. "You're not spending time commuting to work, cooking meals, paying bills, wondering what to wear to work or going out to visit friends. I'd never realised until I stopped doing all those things how much time you spend on them."

On the other hand, the new team is keen to have the chance to be their own bosses for a year in one of the world's most fascinating wildlife areas.

Peter Moore's main work has been with the rare yellow-eyed penguin, checking numbers and following their breeding success, but as he and technician Roger Moffat are the only two working specifically on science projects, he has been given a long "shopping list" of follow-up studies for others.

Every five days, from October to March, Moore and Moffat walked the four kilometres to Northwest Bay to study yellow-eyed penguins. From mid-October to May they walked 14 km to Bull Rock, at the northern end of the island, every 7 to 12 days to study mollymawks. From January to August they

ROGER MOFFAT

Surfing ashore in a tangle of beaks and flippers, dozens of rockhopper penguins return to land after feeding at sea. Rockhoppers breed in colonies of between 5000 and 50,000 on the wave-battered island, but biologists are concerned: there has been a 94 per cent decline in their numbers since the 1940s.

monitored 470 royal albatross nests dotted over the island, counting the eggs and banding surviving chicks. And from November to February they did the same with rockhopper penguins.

During the winter months they spent many lonely hours on the beaches counting the penguins moving to and from the sea. On the way to all these places they picked up feathers for mercury testing, searched for plants wanted by botanists back home and counted fur seals, sea lions and the 1100 sheep.

Moffat lost 15 kg in the first three months of their work and recalls that they were away from base so much "that sometimes we felt like outsiders when we got back there." The rest of the crew welcomed the injection of fresh news into often tired conversations. Said one of the team, "It sure beats hearing someone talk about the generator all the time."

I'm in luck with the weather. The day Moore has agreed to show me around the island is balmy and humid. There is no wind, and at 10 degrees it feels warmer than the miserable Auckland weather I have left behind. Away from the voice of the camp it is quiet—a quietness I can recall only a few times before in my life, in the South Island high country.

Today Campbell Island looks like an idyllic place to live.

Perhaps it was this sort of illusion which made the Government think farming could work on Campbell Island, for in 1895 Campbell was leased to a Gisborne sheep farmer. He set about building a house, woolshed and store at Tucker Cove. You would hardly know it now, except for the coal range which stands incongruously in the tussock.

Life on Campbell soon got the better of the first shepherds, and even specially recruited Shetland Islanders couldn't face the isolation. Tory Channel whalers who tended sheep when they weren't harpooning right whales lasted from 1909 to 1916.

The last shepherds and leaseholders were lucky to get off Campbell during the Depression. Only lobbying by relatives of the men finally forced the government to send a ship for them. By that time they were using raw sheep hides for boots and surviving on a diet of mutton, tea and the odd shag.

Walking on Campbell Island is the strangest experience. Much of the island's surface is peat—metres deep in places. As we walk it quivers. I notice what look like small rabbit holes riddling the peat. Moore explains that they are rat holes. The island is plagued with Norway rats which came ashore from the ships of whalers and sealers early last century.

At the last estimate there were 100,000 of them. Their main diet is plants and insects, but they have also virtually eliminated burrowing birds from the main island by eating the chicks. Only 50 of the flightless Campbell Island teal now survive, restricted to tiny Dent Island, 2 km offshore.

To reach the royal albatross breeding grounds we first have to walk through the island's distinctive *Dracophyllum* scrub— five metres high and the nearest thing to forest the island has.

There is only one real tree on Campbell Island, a sitka spruce planted early this century by a hopeful Earl of Ranfurly, a former Governor-General. It's no great success as a specimen, and after all these years is only 7.5 m high. But it has gained distinction in the *Guinness Book of Records* as the "loneliest tree on earth."

However, it is the megaherbs, the giant herbaceous plants of Campbell, that astound and delight those who visit here. In summer, large parts of the island are covered with these brilliantly coloured plants. The yellow lilies, *Bulbinella rossii*, are so bright that an early botanist, Sir Joseph Hooker, mentioned them as "giving a yellow tinge to the landscape clearly visible 2 km from the shore."

One giant, waist-high herb of the carrot family, *Anisotome latifolia*, has mauve flowers; another, *Stilbocarpa polaris*, with its green-yellow flowers, helped save the lives of castaways on Disappointment Island in the Auckland Islands after their ship was wrecked in 1907. They baked the roots of the plant, then peeled them and ate them like potatoes.

At length we reach the world's largest seabirds, royal albatrosses with wings up to 3.3 metres across. From a distance, the chicks look slightly ludicrous, dotted at carefully spaced distances, their large heads peering at us over the tussock. These birds are from last December's eggs. Now they are full-sized, although some still have fluffy down clinging to their otherwise immaculate necks.

In a few weeks they will leave the island, and for four years will circle the Southern Hemisphere before coming home again, first to visit, later to nest and produce their own chicks. When they arrive back at Campbell they will not be able to walk for a few days.

The returning birds will not produce their first chicks until they are eight to ten years old, but once they mate they will usually stay with the same partner for life. And life for royal albatrosses can be a long time. One northern albatross at Taiaroa Head on the Otago Peninsula is at least 61 years old.

The island is home to five species of albatross. But it is the light-mantled sooty albatross which has a special place in the hearts of the people who have lived there.

Today, on his last walk over the island, Roger Moffat's scientific matter-of-factness disappears into boyish excitement when he sees the first sooty of the season—returned home after thousands of miles flying around the Southern Ocean. For years now, the sooties have arrived home on the same dates each year. With their soft purple-grey heads and distinctive semi-circle of white around their eyes, these sensuous birds fly tandem with their mates in an uncanny, perfect unison. And they share an eerie, echoing call which you never forget once you've heard it. For some it seems to epitomise the haunting quality of the island itself.

As we walk on I can hardly believe how approachable and unafraid all the birds and animals are. Around the shores of

PETER MOORE

The elevated nests of mollymawks keep eggs and chicks away from the cold, wet peat, and also make a convenient seat for science technician Roger Moffat, who has the task of measuring the birds.

Tucker Cove two sea lion pups follow us like watery spaniels, rolling and splashing along the water line two metres away. I kneel on a rock to have a closer look and one comes right out of the water to inspect me before yawning a wide, brown-toothed malodorous sigh and sinking back into the water.

There are still the remains of whaling operations at Capstan Cove, where the Tory Channel whalers winched the animals ashore to butcher them. The southern right, considered the "right" whales for hunting, were killed for their oil and baleen—the three-metre long curtain of flexible bone plates between their jaws through which they sieve their food. Their baleen was used as corset stays, riding crops and umbrella ribs. Between 1909 and 1916 more than 60 whales died here. Now with total protection, their numbers are slowly growing, and one of the tasks for staff during their year's stay is whalewatching.

The *Dracophyllum* behind Middle Bay, one of the small

PETER MOORE

Juvenile yellow-eyed penguin— one of the rarest penguins in the world— rests among the bright flowers of the Bulbinella *lily and the lichen-coated trunks of* Dracophyllum *scrub.*

bays in Northwest Bay, is crisscrossed by tracks—narrow, deep, mud-filled tracks with steep, rounded sides—and smaller, tidy little paths which branch into the undergrowth off the main routes. The large tracks are made by sea lions, which lug themselves far up into the hills. Their paths are like hydroslides, and I'm warned that sometimes you have to move very fast to get out of the way when they come down.

The smaller paths are highways where the yellow-eyed penguins walk at sunrise and sunset as they come and go from their nests on their daily fishing trips. Middle Bay is the

breeding ground which Moore and Moffat have been studying for 12 months. While the little rockhopper penguins, the "punk rockers" of the penguin world with their spiked, yellow-tasselled heads and their geranium-red eyes, prefer to live in the teeth of gales at the western end of the island, the yellow-eyeds prefer the relative shelter of the bays and the *Dracophyllum.*

The rockhoppers are garrulous birds which like being together. They come ashore in their hundreds in a great commotion of foamy waves, flippers and feet, then crowd together on their rocky homes, squabbling in voices so loud that a base member describes the noise as sounding like a construction site.

Yellow-eyed penguins, on the other hand, are loners, preferring not to see each other when they're nesting. So every five days Moore and Moffat had to crawl through the *Dracophyllum* and the sheep and bird excrement to visit the 40 scattered study nests. "We got pretty good at it after a while," Moore says, "We had the area mapped out; turn right here, so many paces to this nest, turn left there . . . you can usually smell them anyway."

The work told on the men's bodies. Even in summer, during the wet and cold weather Moore's hands were covered in cuts, and Moffat's knees caused him problems. More mature chicks would wander away from home, which meant the two men had to crawl in ever-increasing circles looking for them. Parent J9170 was such a vicious kneebiter that its chick was eventually excluded from the study.

Moore estimates that there are probably about 2000 yellow-eyed penguins on the island, and they seem to be doing well. And that's the biggest difference between the rockhoppers and these birds, for the rockhopper numbers are decreasing so markedly that scientists are very concerned.

In fact, the picture is not good for a number of animals on Campbell Island. There has been a severe decline in elephant seals and in two of the albatross family—the New Zealand black-browed and grey-headed mollymawks. Photographs of the mollymawk colonies in the 1940s showed thousands of birds; now there are just a handful in some colonies.

One possible explanation is that sea temperatures have warmed by a degree and a half over the last 40 years, and this could be driving krill—an important component of many diets—further south. I find myself wondering whether, given the cutbacks in spending, scientists will ever be able to finish the work needed to definitively answer the questions.

As the *Daniel Solander* pulls out at dusk, dozens of penguins on their way home for the night leap out of the water. The seven people we are leaving buzz the ship in their small boat in a cocky show of bravado. Then, as the ship moves up the harbour towards the boisterous Southern Ocean, we watch them turn back to take up their solitary 12-month custodianship of this special island.

ROGER MOFFAT

On a clear day Campbell Island looks every inch a paradise for nature-lovers. Clumps of giant flowering plants cling to the soaring clifftops, albatrosses wheel and cry, and the wild Southern Ocean relentlessly batters the shores.

THE AUTHOR

KENNEDY WARNE is the founding editor of *New Zealand Geographic* magazine. Under his leadership, the journal has become a forum for writing and photography which examines and celebrates the nation's cultural and geographical identity. Warne graduated MSc (Hons.) in zoology in 1978, and worked in publishing, advertising and public relations before co-launching *New Zealand Geographic* in 1989.

ACKNOWLEDGMENTS

New Zealand Geographic gratefully acknowledges all who have helped make possible the publication of this volume, particularly the individuals and organisations named, portrayed or quoted in its pages, the contributors who made their work available for re-publication, and the many people who helped during the production of the original articles. Kennedy Warne is especially grateful to Vaughan Yarwood, Warren Judd and Arno Gasteiger for helping refine the concept and structure of the book, and to John Woods, the magazine's founding publisher, for dreaming up the idea of "New Zealand's own" *Geographic* in the first place.